LEMON
TWIST:
NO SALT ADDED
COOKBOOK

Zesty and Zingy
Lemon Recipes, Garnishes and Menus

by REE

NUTRITION UNLIMITED PUBLICATIONS

LEMON
TWIST:

NO SALT ADDED
COOKBOOK

(for book ordering information, please turn to last page)

Published by

Nutrition Unlimited Publications
P.O. Box 701
Arcadia, California 91006

First Edition

Printed in the United States of America

Copyright 1989 by Ruth M. H. Reeder

Library of Congress
Catalogue Card Number: 87-92238
ISBN: 0-929622-00-6

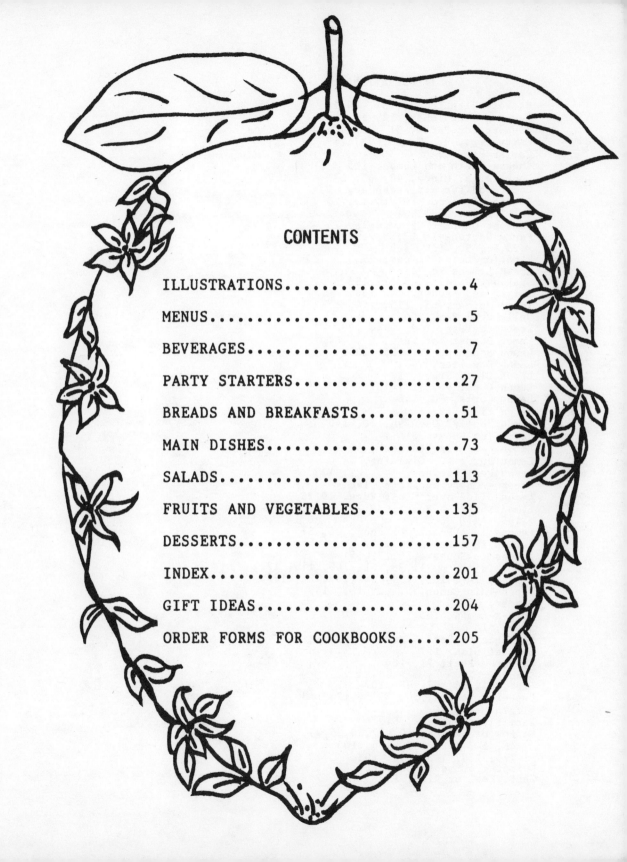

CONTENTS

ILLUSTRATIONS

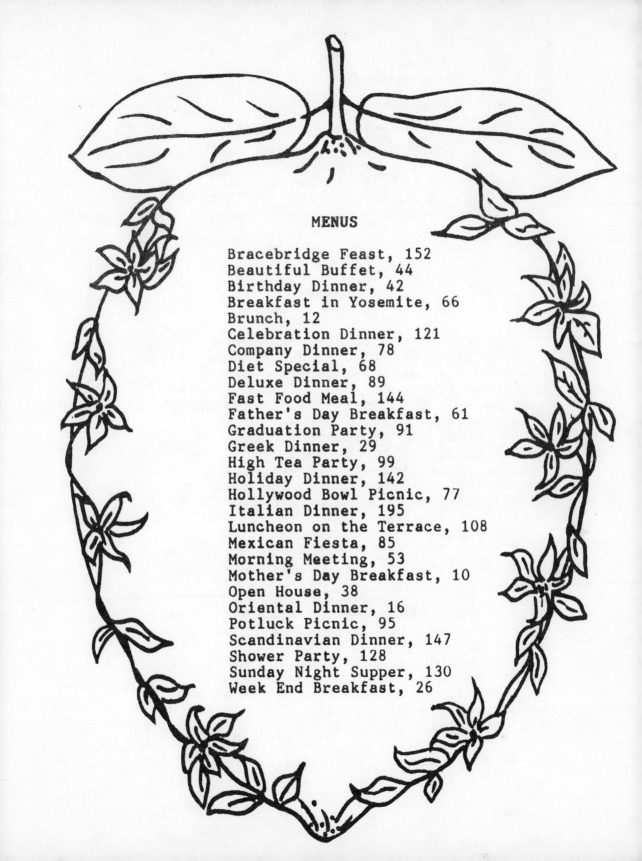

MENUS

DEDICATION

I dedicate this book to my husband, Bill, for his sustaining love and support with this endeavor.

R.H.R.

FOREWORD

Inspired by the bounty and potential of the California lemon, no kitchen is complete without this classic cookbook.

Choose from over 200 kitchen tested recipes. This book is generously illustrated by over 100 "How to use the lemon" drawings to present food in a beautiful way. With 28 menus for every occasion from elegant dinner-party fare to sumptuous picnic treats, you will win compliments when you entertain indoors or out.

For a uniquely perfect gift anytime, give Lemon Twist: No Salt Added Cookbook with any of the 40 gift ideas in this book.

In the best interest of your health lemon is the seasoning. No salt has been added to any recipes. Nutritional and historical notes have been included to further emphasize the amazing value of California lemons!

Our best effort has gone into the book before you. We submit it with pleasure for your health and your joy.

R.H.R.

Beverages

LEMONADE CONCENTRATE

10 lemons, juice and peel
1 cup water
2 cups sugar

After juicing the lemons cut the peel into thin strips. Place in a 13 x 9 pyrex baking dish. Sprinkle with 1 cup sugar and mash with potato masher until the sugar is absorbed.

Dissolve the additional 1 cup sugar in 1 cup boiling water. Put the lemon peel, sugar water, and lemon juice in a covered glass or plastic container. Store in refrigerator or freezer.

LEMONADE

1 cup lemonade concentrate
2 cups ice water
Ice cubes

Remove the soaked, sugared lemon strips from the concentrate to use as garnish. They can be eaten, too!

Place lemonade concentrate, ice water plus ice cubes in blender. Process. Pour into glasses. Garnish with lemon strips, lemon twists, and/or mint leaves.

Makes 4 glasses.

Cut lemon slice to
center and twist.

lemon twist

For Another Twist:
Serve hot lemonade in the winter and cold lemonade in the summer.

PINK LEMONADE

1 cup lemon juice
3/4 cup sugar
4 cups water
1 or 2 drops red food coloring
Ice Cubes
1 lemon for cartwheels*

Dissolve sugar in 1 cup very hot water. In large pitcher, combine lemon juice, sugar, water and food coloring. Fill glasses with ice. Pour lemonade over ice. Cut a cartwheel to the middle. Slip cartwheel over the edge of glass.

Makes 6 cups.

*Cartwheels: Slice unpeeled lemon crosswise, about 1/4 inch thick.

Cartwheel variations: Notch edge with shears or paring knife...Slice in half and stud with cloves...Decorate with sliced stuffed olives, chopped parsley, sprigs of mint or parsley, celery leaves, maraschino cherries, small blossoms or fresh berries.

"Lemons contain Vitamins B, C, P, and niacin."
Funk Wagnalls, 1983

NO SUGAR LEMONADE

1 cup lemon juice (5 lemons)
8 envelopes Equal (each equal to 2
   teaspoons sugar)
8 cups ice water
1 lemon, sliced in cartwheels
Ice cubes

In large pitcher, combine lemon juice
and Equal. Stir to dissolve Equal. Add
remaining ingredients. Blend well. Serve
over ice. Garnish with a lemon cartwheel.

Makes 6 cups.

MOTHER'S DAY BREAKFAST

Orange Smiles
French Toast and Topping
No Sugar Lemonade and Non Fat Milk
A red rose

indicates it can be found in the index

INVENTION OF LEMONADE

A drop in the price of West Indian
sugar inspired the invention, in Paris in
1630, of lemonade. Owners of the sidewalk
cafes of Paris became known as
limonadiers.

A "NO" DRINK WITH A LEMON TWIST
(no calories, no caffeine, no alcohol)

Club Soda
Ice cubes
Lemon Twist

Pour club soda over ice cubes and add a lemon twist.

Makes 1 serving.

A LEMON TWIST

1. Use plain or notched cartwheel.
2. Make one cut into cartwheel from edge of peel to center.
3. Twist ends in opposite directions, standing cartwheel gently.
4. Use plain or decorate with paprika, parsley or mint.

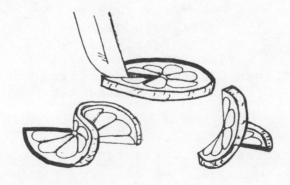

MINT JULIAS

1/2 cup sugar
1 cup water
2 cups orange juice
1 cup lemon juice
1 (8 ounce) can crushed pineapple
4 ripe bananas, mashed
1 quart lemon lime or club soda
Mint leaves
Lemon Twists
Long Picks

Dissolve sugar in very hot water. Cool. Add orange and lemon juices, undrained crushed pineapple, and mashed bananas. Stir well. Freeze in plastic container or muffin tins (remove when frozen and store in plastic bags). About 10 minutes before serving remove from freezer to thaw slightly. Place a mint leaf and 3 scoops of frozen mixture in large stemmed glass. Fill with chilled lemon lime or soda. Garnish with skewered lemon twists and mint on long picks.

Makes about 10 servings.

BRUNCH

*Mint Julias
Tijuana Quiche
*Piroshiki
*Ice Berg Bran Muffins
*Lemon Glazed Apricot Cheese Buns
*Finger Food Fruits and Dip

*(denotes that these recipes are in this book)

COFFEE MEXICO

1/2 cup cocoa mix
1 teaspoon grated lemon rind
1 drop aromatic bitters (Angostura)
Hot brewed coffee
*Whipped topping

Combine cocoa mix, lemon rind and bitters, mix well. For each serving of coffee, place about 1-1/2 teaspoons cocoa mixture in cup or mug, pour in coffee. Add a dollop of *whipped topping(see index)

Makes 6 servings.

Note: The cocoa mixture stores well in the refrigerator in a jar or container with tight-fitting lid.

Garnish with twisted lemon peel and cherry on a long pick.

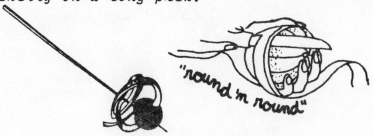

"round 'n round"

Round 'n Round
Round 'n Round with a slightly sawing motion, cut the peel away in a continuous spiral.

CAFE DIABLE

1/3 cup sugar
1/8 teaspoon ground bay leaf
2 teaspoons grated orange peel
1/2 teaspoon grated lemon peel
Hot brewed coffee

Combine sugar, bay leaf, orange and lemon peel. Mix well. For each serving, use about 1-1/2 teaspoons citrus peel mixture for each cup of coffee.

Citrus peel mixture can be stored for later use in the refrigerator in a jar with tight-fitting lid.

Makes 8 servings.

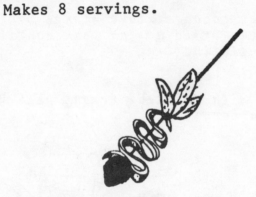

Nutrition in the Peel

"The outer peel of the lemon contains oil of lemon. The white layer beneath it contains citrin.

Concentrated lemon juice is used medicinally for its high Vitamin C content."

Funk, Wagnalls, 1983

COFFEE NAPOLI

1/2 cup coffee grounds
2 tablespoons grated lemon peel
2 tablespoons grated orange peel
1 teaspoon anise seed
6 cups water
*whipped topping (see index)

Combine coffee, lemon and orange peel plus the anise seed in brew basket of automatic drip coffee maker. Prepare coffee with 6 cups water. Serve in small cups with a garnish of whipped topping and grated lemon peel on top.

Makes 12 servings in after dinner coffee cups.

Grated peel enhances many beverages.

*Wash fruit. Dry. With quick downward strokes, remove outer colored layer of peel only. (This is sometimes called rind or zest as well as peel) Grate over waxed paper. Measure **lightly** in spoon. Do not pack.*

PERFECT CUPPA TEA

1 tea bag for 3 cups water
Lemon cartwheels
Milk
*Lemon Sugar

Bring cold water to a boil. If using a tea pot, rinse first with boiling water to warm. Place teabag(s) in warmed tea pot or in individual cups. Pour boiling water over tea bags. Cover to contain flavor. Steep for 10 minutes in tea pot or one minute in cup. Remove teabag(s).
Serve with lemon cartwheels, lemon sugar, and milk.

Makes 3 cups per tea bag.

ORIENTAL DINNER

*Perfect Cuppa Tea
*Shrimps in Lobster Sauce
Spareribs with *Best Barbecue Sauce
Egg Foo Yung
Pea Pods and Water Chestnuts with *Lemon Twist
Chow Mein Noodles
*Perfection Salad (add bean sprouts)
Fortune Cookies   Almond Cookies
* Orange Smiles
*Lemony Rice Pudding

Lemon Helps Calcium Intake
Tea, especially instant tea, will inhibit the absorption of calcium. However, if you use lemon in tea calcium will be absorbed by your body.*
*Dr. Dean Edell, ABC-Eye Witness News, 5/23/88

CROCK POT WASSAIL

3 cups apple cider
4 cups orange juice
1 teaspoon lemon peel
1-1/2 cups lemon juice
4 cups water
1 cup brown sugar
3/4 cup granulated sugar
1 stick cinnamon
1/4 teaspoon whole cloves
1/4 teaspoon nutmeg

In large crock pot heat cider, juices, sugar, and cinnamon stick to boiling. Reduce heat. Cover and simmer 5 minutes. Uncover and stir in remaining ingredients. Simmer 5 minutes longer. Serve from crock pot to keep hot and handy. Float lemon clove stars on top.

Makes 16 punch cup servings.

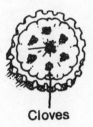

Cloves

LEMON CLOVE STARS
Cut lemons into 1/4 inch slices. Insert 7 cloves at equal intervals in edge of each slice and one in the middle.

FRIENDSHIP TEA

1-1/3 cups Orange Flavor Powdered
   Beverage Drink
1/2 cup sugar
1/3 cup instant lemon flavored tea
1/2 teaspoon cinnamon
1/4 teaspoon cloves

Prepare a mix by combining the above ingredients.
   Store in tightly covered jars.
   This recipe can be doubled or tripled. It makes a nice gift when put in an attractive container. Include the recipe and directions.

Makes 50 servings.

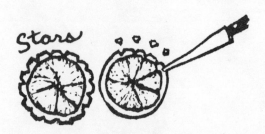

DIRECTIONS

For 1 serving: place 1 well rounded teaspoon of mix in a cup, fill with boiling water and stir until dissolved.

For 1 quart(6 servings): dissolve 1/3 cup of the mix in 1 quart boiling water in a heatproof pitcher or crock pot.

Serve it hot with a lemon star in each cup.

CATALINA ICED TEA

3 quarts of water
1/2 cup tea leaves
1 cup sugar
1 cup water
1 cup lemon juice
4 sprigs of fresh mint

Bring 3 quarts of water to a boil and pour over tea in a large pot. Let steep 5 minutes. Add 1 cup of water to lemon juice and sugar. Bring to a boil. Strain tea into juices and sugar. Add mint. Stir and refrigerate. This tea keeps well without clouding for 3-4 days in refrigerator.

Makes 16 servings. (Most people want refills it is so good!)

Get more juice from lemons by microwaving 20 seconds on high before cutting and squeezing.

SPARKLING CIDER

4 cups apple cider
1/4 cup lemon juice
1 quart club soda, chilled

Combine apple and lemon juice. Chill. Just before serving add club soda. Pour into frosted glasses. Drop in a twist of lemon peel.

Makes 12 servings.

LEMON PEEL TWIST

Twist a "twist" of lemon peel before dropping into your favorite beverages. Twisting the peel releases fragrant lemon oils.

Snacker: For perfect lemon twists or ease in peeling oranges.

LYNN'S SPECIAL SLUSHY PUNCH

3 cups sugar
6 cups water
1 (46 ounce) can pineapple juice
5 ripe bananas, mashed
2 (6 ounce) cans frozen lemonade
  plus water as directed
2 (12 ounce) cans frozen orange
  juice plus water as directed
4 (quart) bottles lemon lime or
  club soda

Dissolve sugar in 6 cups water. Combine all the juices (plus water as directed). Add bananas which have been mashed in blender with some of the juice.

Freeze this mixture in jello rings or molds.
Thaw approximately 1 hour prior to serving. Place in punch bowl. Add equal parts of soda just before serving. Stir to mix.

Makes 50 servings.

This punch base keeps well in freezer. It is great to have on hand.
When you have over ripe bananas mash them and add a little lemon juice. Freeze it to use later in this punch or in banana bread.

NO PROBLEM WEDDING PUNCH

1 cup lemon juice
3 cups orange juice
1 cup pineapple juice
1 (12 ounce) bottle apricot juice
1-1/4 cups granulated sugar
1 cup hot water
3 cups double-strength hot tea
3 quarts carbonated lemon lime
Lemon Ice Ring

Dissolve sugar in hot water and tea. Combine with fruit juices. Chill. Just before serving, add chilled carbonated beverage and lemon ice ring to punch base in the punch bowl.

Makes 40 punch cup servings.

LEMON ICE RING

1 lemon, sliced in thin cartwheels
1 orange, sliced in half-cartwheels
Green leaves (mint or parsley)

Fill a 1-1/2 quart ring mold or bundt pan 1/2 full with water. Freeze until firm. Arrange citrus slices and green leaves on top of ice ring. Fill to 3/4 full with water. Freeze until firm. Just before serving place mold briefly in warm water. Remove ice ring. Float it in punch bowl.
Decorate around punch bowl with endive, baby's breath and fresh flowers.

LEMON SHERBET PUNCH

2 quarts cider, chilled
1 quart lemon sherbet
1 quart gingerale

Scoop sherbet into punch bowl. Pour cider or juice over the sherbet.
Just before serving, add gingerale. Garnish with sprigs of mint and strawberries around punch bowl.

Makes 20 servings.

LEMON SHERBET
(1 quart)
1 can (6 ounces) frozen lemonade
  concentrate
4 drops yellow food color
1 can (13 ounces) evaporated milk,
  chilled

Beat chilled milk until stiff. Stir in lemonade concentrate and food color. Pour into 2 refrigerator trays. Freeze until firm.

Makes 8 servings.

Beverage Garnishes

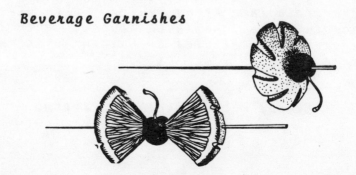

MOCK BUTTERMILK

1 tablespoon lemon juice
1 cup milk

Mix together and let stand 5 minutes.
Serve ice cold.
This can be used in recipes that
require buttermilk or sour milk.

Makes 1 serving.

*Juicer and Faucet: Two quick ways to
squeeze lemon juice.*

FROSTED GLASSES

To frost and chill glasses dip rim of
each glass into lemon juice, then into
granulated or powdered sugar. Put in
freezer a few minutes to harden sugar and
frost glass.

Lemons make everything lively.

CANDY CANE PUNCH

1/2 cup lemon juice
1 (6-ounces) can frozen orange juice
6 crushed candy canes
1 quart Ginger-ale or Club Soda

Put all ingredients except soda in blender. Cover and process. Divide evenly between four tall glasses. Add soda slowly just before serving. Stir to mix.

Serve with candy canes as stirrers, if desired.

Makes 4 servings.

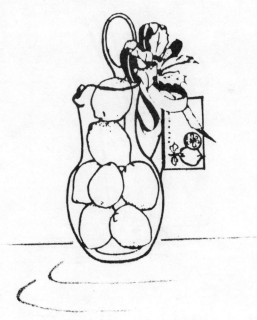

Nice gift. . . . .
include the Lemon Twist Cook Book!

VIRGIN MARY

2 tablespoons lemon juice
2-1/2 cups tomato juice
1 teaspoon Worcestershire sauce
1/2 teaspoon instant minced onion
4 celery stalks

Combine tomato juice, lemon juice, and Worcestershire sauce. Chill. Serve with a stalk of celery in each glass. Garnish with a slice of lemon on the edge of the glass.

Makes 4 servings.

WEEK END BREAKFAST

*Virgin Mary
*Pineapple Sauce with Ham
*German Pancakes
*Mincemeat Coffee Cake

Party
Starters

BOUILLON SIPPER

2 (10-1/2 ounce) cans condensed beef
   bouillon
1 soup can water
1 tablespoon barbecue sauce
5 notched edge lemon cartwheels
1 tablespoon minced parsley

Combine bouillon, water and barbecue
sauce in saucepan. Add lemon slices. Heat
thoroughly. Serve in mugs. Put a paper
thin lemon cartwheel sprinkled with
parsley in each mug.

Makes 5 servings.

*Famous American hostess, Dolly Madison,
served bouillon in mugs to her guests when
they arrived on cold evenings.*

NOTCHED EDGE CARTWHEELS
*Hold stem end and blossom end of lemon
with thumb and middle finger. Score peel
from end to end leaving about 1/2 inch
between each cut. Cut paper thin slices to
make cartwheels. Decorate with chopped
parsley.*

FLOATING LEMON SOUP

1 can tomato soup
1 can evaporated milk
6 tiny broccoli florets
6 thin lemon slices

Heat soup and milk until hot. Divide soup evenly into 2 bowls. Float 3 lemon slices in each. Top each lemon slice with a broccoli floret.

Makes 2 servings.

GREEK DINNER

*Floating Lemon Soup
*Cabbage Babies
*Peas and Carrots
*Nippy Beet Salad
*Baklava

CHILLED GAZPACHO SOUP

1 (46 ounce) can tomato juice
1 medium green pepper, minced
1 small onion, minced
1 cucumber, peeled and minced
2 small canned green chiles, minced
1 tablespoon Worcestershire sauce
1/2 teaspoon minced garlic
1 tablespoon olive oil
1 tablespoon chopped chives
2 drops tabasco sauce
1/4 teaspoon white pepper
8 lemon smiles

Combine tomato juice, green pepper, onion, cucumber, chiles, Worcestershire, garlic, olive oil, chives and tabasco sauce. Season to taste with white pepper and lemon juice. Chill thoroughly. Serve with lemon smiles.

Makes 8 servings.

. lovely soup for a patio supper after a hot day...

Smile: it takes fewer calories to obtain Vitamin C from lemon juice than from orange juice.

LEMON TREE SOUP

3 avocados
3/4 cup lemon juice
3 cups vegetable bouillon
1-1/2 cups sour cream

Puree avocados with lemon juice and bouillon. Add half of the sour cream. After chilling thoroughly, garnish with the remainder of sour cream.

Makes 8 servings.

MOCK SOUR CREAM

1 tablespoon lemon juice
1 cup creamed cottage cheese

Process in blender until smooth and creamy. Mock Sour Cream is higher in protein, lower in calories and just as good as sour cream! The recipe may be doubled.

Makes 1 cup.

SCURVY AND VITAMIN C

"Vitamin C in lemons has been used for centuries against, scurvy, a disease marked by spongy gums, loosening of the teeth, and a bleeding into the skin and mucous membranes, all caused by a lack of ascorbic acid.
If we exclude straight forward famine, scurvy is probably the nutritional deficiency disease that has caused the most suffering in recorded history."

Excerpts from The History of Scurvy and Vitamin C (Cambridge University Press), by Kenneth Carpenter, since 1977 a professor of nutrition at Berkeley.

SWEDISH FRUIT SOUP

1 cup dried apricots
1 cup pitted prunes
1/2 cup raisins
6 cups water
1/2 lemon, sliced
1 cinnamon stick
1/2 teaspoon cloves
1/2 cup sugar
1/2 orange, peeled and diced
1 apple, peeled and diced
3 tablespoons cornstarch
8 lemon wedges

In large saucepan, combine all ingredients except cornstarch and lemon wedges. Heat to boiling. Cover and simmer 10 minutes.

Dissolve constarch in a 1/4 cup of cold water. Gradually stir into fruit mixture. Cook until mixture thickens slightly and begins to boil. Remove cinnamon and lemon. Discard. Serve warm or cold. To serve, ladle into individual bowls. Garnish with lemon wedges dipped in cinnamon or nutmeg.

Makes 8 servings.

This is excellant served as a starter or as a meat accompaniment as well as a dessert.

unpeeled wedges

MOCK TURTLE SOUP

2 cups dry black beans
1/4 cup chopped onion
1/4 cup margarine
2 stalks celery
10 cups boiling water
1/4 cup lemon juice
2 hard-cooked eggs, chopped
1 lemon thinly sliced

Soak beans in water overnight. Drain. Cook onion in margarine until soft. Add beans and onion to celery in water. Cook until beans are tender. Put through blender or food processor to puree. Add lemon juice and heat to warm. Garnish with hard-cooked eggs and lemon slices sprinkled with capers or parsley.

Makes 8 servings.

(Turtle Soup was a favorite recipe of President Monroe's.)

U.S. RDA

To help Americans plan meals that will meet their nutritional needs, the Food And Drug Administration developed guidelines called the United States Recommended Daily Allowances (U.S. RDA) for all Americans over the age of four.

The U.S. RDA Requirement for Vitamin C (Ascorbic Acid) is 60 milligrams.

1 lemon has 46 milligrams (Ascorbic Acid) Vitamin C.*

*Agriculture Handbook No.456, Nutritive Value of American Foods, Agricultural Research Service, United States Department of Agriculture, 1975.

MULLIGATAWNY SOUP

3 tablespoons margarine
2 cups chopped onion
2 cups seeded, chopped tart apples
3 cloves garlic, minced
3 teaspoons curry powder
6 cups chicken bouillon
1 (4 pound) chicken, skinned
1/4 pound veal, cut in 1/4" cubes
1/2 teaspoon pepper
1/4 cup corn starch
1/4 cup water
1/4 cup lemon juice

In 8 quart saucepan melt margarine. Add onion, apples, garlic, curry powder. Cook 5 minutes until tender. Add bouillon, chicken, veal and pepper. Cover. Simmer 1 hour or until chicken is tender. Remove chicken. Discard bones. Cut chicken into 1" pieces. Mix corn starch and water. Add to soup. Stir constantly. Bring to boil. Boil 1 minute. Add lemon juice and chicken. Serve with boiled rice.

Makes 10 servings.

Use a lemon wedge in chilled water to add zest.

CHAFING DISH SCAMPI

2 pounds medium, raw shrimp
1/4 cup margarine
1/4 cup olive oil
2 tablespoons minced parsley
3/4 teaspoon basil
1/2 teaspoon oregano
1 garlic clove minced
1 teaspoon lemon juice

Shell, clean and devein shrimp, leaving tails on. Split shrimp almost through down center. Melt margarine and add oil in a chafing dish over direct heat, then add remaining ingredients.
Place shrimp in chafing dish, bring sauce to a boil. Cover. Cook 8 minutes or just until shrimp are pink. Put top pan of chafing dish over hot water. Cover and keep warm. Provide toothpicks and napkins for those who wish to use their fingers!

Makes 3 to 4 servings.

Serve with a Smile!
For lemon smiles cut unpeeled lemon in half. Cut 2 or more "smiles" from each half. Remove seeds. These are perfect for squeezing on shrimp. Also, after handling fish rub your hands with a lemon smile and it will take away the odor.

TUNA ALMONDINE

2 envelopes unflavored gelatin
1/2 cup cold water
1 cup boiling water
2 (8 ounce) blocks cream cheese,
   softened
1 avocado, peeled and mashed
3 tablespoons lemon juice
1 tablespoon curry powder
1/4 teaspoon garlic powder
1/3 cup finely chopped green onions
1/2 cup red pepper
2 cans (7 ounce) tuna, drained
1-1/4 cups sliced almonds

In large bowl, sprinkle unflavored gelatin over cold water. Let stand 1 minute. Add boiling water and stir until gelatin is completely dissolved. Blend in cream cheese and avocado until smooth. Stir in lemon juice, curry powder, and garlic powder. Fold in green onions, 1/4 cup chopped red pepper, tuna and 1/2 cup almonds. Turn into 5-1/2 cup fish mold or French bread pan. Chill until firm. To serve, unmold onto platter. Garnish with remaining almonds, overlapping to form scales, green olive slices for eyes, parsley for lashes, red pepper strips for mouth and tail fins. Serve with crackers or party breads.

Makes about 5-1/2 cups.

Aluminum and Lemons
To prevent the discoloration of lemon in foods, avoid putting the food in contact with aluminum foil or uncoated aluminum cookware.

HOT CURRIED LEMONY TUNA OR CRAB DIP

1 package (8 ounce) soft cream cheese
1 can (6 ounce) tuna or crab, drained
1 tablespoon lemon juice
1 tablespoon onion grated
1/8 teaspoon curry
1/8 teaspoon Tabasco sauce
1/4 teaspoon paprika
3 lemon twists

Combine cream cheese, lemon juice, onion, curry, and Tabasco. Stir with fork until blended. Add tuna or crab. Bake in 350 degree oven 20 to 25 minutes, or until hot and bubbly. Garnish with lemon slices and paprika. Serve with raw vegetables or crackers.

Microwave Method: Prepare as above. Microwave on high 4 to 5 minutes or until hot. Stir half way through. Let stand 2 minutes before serving.

Makes 8 servings.

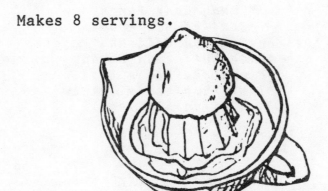

Lemon juice is an appetite suppressant if taken before a meal.

STUFFED MUSHROOMS

18 medium mushrooms
1 package (3 ounces) cream cheese
1/4 cup onion
1/4 cup green pepper
1/4 cup celery
1/ cup margarine
1 cup bread crumbs
1 tablespoon lemon juice

Rinse mushrooms and pat dry. Remove stems. Set caps aside. Saute onion, green pepper, and celery in margarine until soft. Mix with cream cheese, bread crumbs and lemon juice. Stuff mushroom caps and heat in microwave on high for 3 minutes.

Makes 18 stuffed mushrooms.

HOLIDAY OPEN HOUSE

*Candy Cane Punch
*Stuffed Mushrooms
*Festive Salmon Ball and Veggies
*Date Nut Lemon Bread
*Pineapple Lemon Loaf
*Tom Thumb Lemon Tarts
*Friendship Tea

lemon peel holly garnish

see P. 64

AVOCADO DIP

2 large ripe avocados
3 tablespoons lemon juice
1 (4 ounce)can diced chilies
1 tablespoon minced onion

Mash peeled avocados. Add remaining ingredients and blend well. Refrigerate one hour before serving. Stuff hard boiled egg white shells with dip. Garnish plate with lemon twists decorated with paprika.

Makes 2 cups.

DILL DIP

1 container (16 ounces) large curd
   cottage cheese
4 tablespoons fresh lemon juice
1 cup mayonnaise
2 tablespoons dill weed
2 tablespoons chopped parsley
3 tablespoons minced green onions
2 teaspoons beaumont seasoning

Mix all ingredients. Chill at least one hour before serving. Serve with veggies cut a convenient size for dipping. Serve in a large lemon shell cutting lemon lengthwise and reaming out pulp and juice.

Makes 3-1/2 cups.

lemon shells

FINGER FOOD FRUITS AND DIPS

Apples with lemon water bath
Pears with lemon water bath
Grapes
Bananas with lemon water bath
Peaches with lemon water bath
Melons
Oranges
Pineapple
Strawberries

Wash and slice the fruits. Dip or squirt with lemon water bath to prevent browning with apples, pears, bananas, and peaches. Serve with dips.

Makes 1 serving per 1/2 cup fruit prepared.

LEMON WATER BATH

1/4 cup lemon juice
1 cup water
Combine water and lemon juice. Dip or squirt washed and cut fruit with lemon water bath to prevent browning.

FRUIT DIP

12 ounces cream cheese
1 (9 ounce) can crushed pineapple, drained
3 tablespoons lemon juice
1 teaspoon ground ginger
1 package Angel Flake coconut
6 ounces pecan nuts, chopped

Mix ingredients in order listed. Serve with fruit slices.

Makes 2 cups.

6 LAYER ACAPULCO DIP

2 (10-1/2 ounce) cans bean dip
3 avocados
2 tablespoons lemon juice
1 cup sour cream
1/2 cup mayonnaise
1 cup green onions with tops
8 ounces grated Cheddar Cheese
2 cups chopped tomatoes
7 ounces black olives, chopped
1 package taco seasoning mix
1 cup taco sauce

Spread bean dip over bottom of large round tray. Mash avocados with lemon juice. Layer avocado mixture on top, leaving a border of bean dip. Mix sour cream with mayonnaise. Spread with sour cream mixture, leaving 1/2" avocado border. Sprinkle with at least three of the remaining ingredients. Chill. Serve with tortilla chips.

Makes 16 servings.

Place a cut lemon in the refrigerator for an air freshener.

COCKTAIL SAUCE

1/2 cup ketchup
1/4 cup chili sauce
1/2 lemon with peel, seeded
2 teaspoons horseradish sauce
1/2 teaspoon Worcestershire sauce

Place all ingredients in blender.
Process until smooth.

Makes 3/4 cup sauce.

Great served:
-with Oriental Shrimp Chips
-over a block of cream cheese
  with crackers
-and, of course, as a dunk for
  shrimp, crab or lobster

BIRTHDAY DINNER

*Cocktail Sauce over Block of Cream
Cheese
*Shrimp Chips and Whole Wheat Crackers
*Mock Turtle Soup
*Meat Loaf Wellington
*Steamed Green Beans
*Broiled Tomatoes
*Lemon Pineapple Cheese Salad
*Lemon Cake Roll

CAVIAR PIE

8 hard-cooked eggs, chopped
4 tablespoons mayonnaise
1-1/2 cups finely chopped green onion
1 package (8 ounce) cream cheese
2/3 cup sour cream
1 jar (3-1/2 ounce) black caviar
1 cup chopped parsley
12 lemon wedges

Combine eggs and mayonnaise. Spread in 8 inch spring form pan. Sprinkle chopped green onion over top. Combine cream cheese and sour cream until smooth. Spread over onion with wet spatula. Cover. Chill at least 3 hours.

Just before serving, top with caviar, spreading to the edge of pan. Run knife around sides to loosen pie, then remove sides. Arrange lemon wedges on top and press parsley into sides. Serve with pumpernickel bread or unsalted crackers.

Makes 12 servings.

If desired, make individual servings in egg cups and serve with demi tasse spoons.

MACADAMIA CHEESE BALL

2 packages (8 ounce) cream cheese
1/2 cup margarine
2 tablespoons finely grated onion
1-1/2 cups finely chopped
  Macadamia nuts
2 teaspoons grated lemon peel

Blend cream cheese, margarine and onion. Roll into ball in wax paper and chill several hours. Roll ball in combined nuts and lemon peel. Re-chill until serving time.
Serve with *veggies or crackers.

Makes 1-1/4 pound ball.

Lemon is used in more ways than any other citrus fruit.

BEAUTIFUL BUFFET

*No Problem Wedding Punch
*Macadamia Nut Cheese Ball and *Veggies
*Barbecued Salmon
*Pineapple Sauce with Ham
*Broccoli with Lemon Cream
*Black Cherry Jello
*Lemon Biscuits
*Angel Whispers and *Lemon Fruit Slices
*White Dipped Strawberries
*Coffee Diable

FESTIVE SALMON BALL

1 (16 ounce) can drained salmon
1 (8 ounce) cream cheese, softened
1 tablespoon lemon juice
1 teaspoon grated onion
1 tablespoon white horseradish
1/4 teaspoon paprika
1/2 cup chopped walnuts
3 tablespoons fresh chopped parsley

Thoroughly mix first six ingredients. Roll into ball in wax paper. Chill several hours. Roll ball in combined nuts and parsley.
Re-chill until serving time. Serve with dish of raw vegetables cut into convenient sizes for dipping into salmon ball, or serve with crackers. Salmon ball may be frozen.

Makes 1-3/4 pound ball.

A TWIST ON STORING LEMONS
Store lemons in plastic bags with twisties in the refrigerator for six weeks. To store longer grate the peel, squeeze the juice and freeze in cubes. When frozen put the cubes in plastic bags in the freezer. Label and date!

grated peel

HOT PEPPER COCKTAIL JELLY

2 cups chopped bell peppers
1/2 cup chopped yellow chili peppers
    or green serano peppers
1 cup white vinegar
1/4 teaspoon onion juice
4 cups sugar
1/2 cup strained fresh lemon juice
1 bottle (6 ounces) Certo
Green food coloring

Combine bell peppers, chili peppers and vinegar in blender. Blend until smooth. Pour into saucepan. Add onion juice and sugar. Stir until sugar dissolves. Add lemon juice. Boil 5 minutes. Remove from heat. Add Certo and blend well. Add green food coloring to obtain desired color. Pour into sterilized jars to about 1/4 inch from top.
Top jelly with paraffin or simply use screw-on lid. If refrigerated, the jelly will keep indefinitely. There is no need to "can" according to canning procedures. Jelly may not "gel" immediately but will gel when refrigerated.
*For hotter jelly, do not remove seeds before blending.

Makes 4 cups.

Serve over a block of cream cheese with tortilla chips or whole wheat crackers. Excellent with meats.
Perfect as a hostess gift!

MARINATED ARTICHOKE HEARTS, MUSHROOMS AND TOMATOES

1 (6 ounces) jar artichoke hearts
2 cups mushroom slices
1 cup cherry tomato halves
1/4 cup grated Romano Cheese
1/4 cup chopped parsley
1/2 clove garlic, minced
1 lemon thinly sliced
1/2 cup lemon juice

Combine artichoke hearts, mushrooms, tomatoes and cheese. Toss lightly. Add remaining ingredients. Mix well. Pour over vegetables. Marinate in refrigerator 2 hours or overnight. Drain. Add 1 pound shrimp, if desired. Serve with frilly picks.

Makes 5 cups.

GREEK STYLE

Add 2/3 cup ripe olives and 4 tablespoons feta cheese.

Lemon Juice

To get the full benefit of the lemon, peel and seed the fruit. Cut it in half. Process cut lemon in blender or food processor. Use for juice.

MARINATED MUSHROOMS ORIENTAL

1 pound medium size mushrooms
1/4 cup fresh lemon juice
1/2 cup peanut oil
5 or 6 green onions chopped
1/4 cup chopped parsley
3 tablespoons tarragon vinegar
2 teaspoons sugar
Grape leaves

Clean mushrooms with damp paper toweling. Trim off stems. Place in large bowl and toss with lemon juice. In a smaller bowl, combine other ingredients. Mix well with mushrooms. Refrigerate, stirring occasionally, about 2 or 3 hours. At serving time, skewer each mushroom, bottom side up, with a 6-inch bamboo skewer. Place on a flat plate and circle with grape leaves.

Makes 6 servings.

Don't throw away those marinades after you have drained the mushrooms. Save and use them as a dressing for salads and other vegetables.

To Chop

use both hands

TERIYAKI DRUMETTES

3 pounds chicken wings
1 cup soy sauce
1/2 cup brown sugar
1/2 teaspoon ground ginger
3/4 cup lemon juice

Separate wings at two joints. Discard tips. Place joints in shallow pan. Mix next 4 ingredients. Pour mixture over chicken pieces. Marinate in sauce several hours or overnight in refrigerator. Bake in 350 degree oven for 1-1/4 hours, turning frequently. Drain on paper towels. Serve hot or cold.

Makes 24 servings.

Lemons keep at room temperature for about a week compared to 6 weeks if kept in the refrigerator in plastic bags.

CURRIED CRAB or TUNA CANAPES

2 cups crab or tuna, drained
1 cup shredded white cheese
1 can (8 ounce) water chestnuts,
    drained and chopped.
1/2 cup mayonnaise
1/3 cup chopped green onion
1 clove garlic minced
2 teaspoons lemon juice
1/4 teaspoon curry powder
2 (8 ounce) packages refrigerator
    butterflake rolls
96 almond slices

Preheat oven to 400 degrees. Combine all ingredients except rolls and almond slices.

Separate each roll into 2 layers and place on ungreased cookie sheet. With a small 1 inch lid dipped in flour, stamp an indentation in the center of each roll. Divide crab mixture equally among rolls. Top each with 2 almond slices. Bake 12 minutes or until golden.

Makes 48 servings.

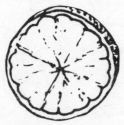

Diet Tip

Weight Watchers recommend 8 to 10 glasses of water a day.
A glass of water with a slice of lemon is a wonderful beverage! Drink it hot or cold.

Breads
and
Breakfasts

MYRNA'S LEMON LOAF

1/2 cup margarine
1 cup sugar
2 eggs, beaten
1 lemon, grated peel
1-1/2 cups flour
1 teaspoon baking powder
1 lemon, grated peel
1/2 cup milk
1/2 cup chopped nuts
1/2 cup chopped dried apricots
*Lemon Pour Topping

Blend margarine and sugar. Add eggs and lemon peel. Sift together flour and baking powder. Add alternately with milk. If desired, stir in nuts and apricots. Turn into greased and wax paper lined 9X5 inch loaf pan. Bake at 350 degrees for 1 hour or until loaf springs back when touched. Let stand in pan 10 minutes, then turn out onto wire rack and pierce top of loaf with fork. Brush with Lemon Pour Topping. Cool before cutting.

LEMON POUR TOPPING
Grated peel and juice of 1 lemon
1/4 cup powdered sugar

Stir sugar and lemon juice until sugar is dissolved.

Makes 1 loaf.

BANANA BREAD

3 ripe medium-sized bananas
2 cups sugar
3 eggs
1 cup soft shortening
1 teaspoon lemon juice
1/2 cup buttermilk
3 cups flour
1 teaspoon baking soda
1 teaspoon baking powder
1/2 cup chopped nuts

Cut the bananas into a mixing bowl. Mash to a smooth liquid using the electric mixer. Add sugar, eggs, and shortening to bananas. Beat until light and smooth.

Blend the buttermilk and lemon juice into the banana mixture. Sift the dry ingredients together and quickly blend with the liquid. Add nuts. Pour into a greased 9 x 13 shiny metal baking pan and bake at 350 for 45 minutes or until a toothpick inserted in the center comes out clean.

Makes 12 servings.

MORNING MEETING

*Lemonade, Regular and No Sugar
*Walnut Wonder Cake
*Banana Bread
*Lemon Tea Loaf
Cream Cheese to spread
Coffee, Tea or Hot Chocolate

DATE NUT LEMON BREAD

2 cups flour
1-1/2 teaspoons baking powder
1/2 teaspoon baking soda
1 cup sugar
1 cup finely chopped nuts
1 package (8 ounces) pitted dates
   cut in eighths
Grated peel and juice of 1 lemon
2 tablespoons margarine, melted
1 egg, well beaten

In mixing bowl, combine first 7 ingredients and mix well. Combine peel, juice, margarine and enough water to make 1-1/2 cups mixture. Beat in egg. Pour over dry ingredients and mix just enough to blend. Spoon into well-greased and lightly floured loaf pan and bake in preheated 325 oven 1 hour and 15 minutes, or until top springs back. Turn out and cool. Wrap airtight and store in cool place. Serve with cream cheese. Keeps about 1 week.

Makes 1 loaf.

CHOLESTEROL BUSTER

For lower cholesterol, margarine is used instead of butter in this book. To pick a good margarine, find a brand that contains at least twice as much polyunsaturated as saturated fatty acids. Look for a P/S ratio of 2-to-1, at least. If the first ingredient on the label is a liquid vegetable oil, you will know the margarine is a cholesterol buster!

PINEAPPLE LEMON LOAF

3 eggs
2 cups sugar
1 cup oil
1/2 cup lemon juice
2 cups peeled, grated zucchini
3 cups flour
1 teaspoon baking powder
1 teaspoon baking soda
1 (8 ounce) can crushed pineapple
   drained
1 cup chopped pecans or walnuts
1 cup raisins

Preheat oven to 350 degrees. Grease and flour 2 (9x5 inch) loaf pans. Beat eggs until fluffy. Add sugar, oil and lemon juice. Add zucchini. Sift together flour, baking powder, soda. Add to batter. Stir in pineapple, nuts and raisins and mix well. Turn into pans. Bake until toothpick inserted in center comes out clean (about 1 hour). Cool on wire rack before removing from pans. Wrap and store overnight to develop flavors before slicing. Zucchini develops the pineapple flavor with lemon. Serve with lemon butter.

Makes 2 loaves.

LEMON BUTTER
Combine 1/2 cup margarine, grated peel and juice of 1/2 lemon.

MONKEY BREAD

4 packages refrigerated buttermilk
  biscuits
1/2 pound margarine, melted
4 teaspoons grated lemon peel
1 cup sugar

Mix lemon peel with sugar. Separate biscuits, divide in half and dip each into margarine then into lemon sugar to coat. Place one layer in bottom of bundt pan, slightly overlapping each biscuit. Arrange remaining biscuits in a zig-zag overlapping fashion, some toward center and some toward outside edge of pan. Use all biscuits and make as many layers as needed. Bake in 375 degree oven 40 minutes or until knife inserted in center comes out clean. Invert on serving platter and pour remaining margarine and lemon sugar over bread. This recipe can be cut in half. Bake in a pie pan or loaf pan. Serve warm or cold.

Makes 24 servings.

Variations

Cinnamon Sugar: dip biscuits in melted margarine and then into a mixture of 1 cup sugar and 3 teaspoons cinnamon. Proceed as above.

Herbs: dip biscuits in melted margarine and then into a mixture of herbs (basil, dill, parsley or other herbs). Proceed as above.

Monkey bread is named because it is broken apart when served. Monkey's don't have thumbs. They can not cut with a knife.

FROSTED SANDWICH LOAF

1 loaf bread cut lengthwise or
1 loaf sandwich bread
1/4 pound soft margarine
2 (8 ounce) packages cream cheese
5 tablespoons milk
8 lemon cartwheels
1 green pepper

Egg Salad Filling
4 hard cooked eggs, chopped
3 tablespoons mayonnaise
2 teaspoons prepared mustard
2 drops yellow food coloring

Ham Filling
1 cup ground cooked ham
1/3 cup mayonnaise
1 tablespoon chopped green pepper
1 teaspoon prepared horseradish

Chicken Filling
1 cup cooked, diced chicken
1/4 cup chopped celery
1/4 cup mayonnaise
2 tablespoons pimiento

Combine ingredients for fillings. Trim crusts from bread. Spread with margarine. Arrange 4 slices, margarine side up with ends touching or 1 long layer of bread. Spread with egg salad filling. Top with bread. Spread with ham filling. Top with more bread. Spread with chicken filling. Repeat. End with bread; margarine side down. Wrap loaf in plastic wrap. Chill.

Blend cream cheese with milk. Frost loaf. Chill. To decorate with a "Daisy" on top of loaf use lemon cartwheels and green pepper for stem and leaves.

Makes 12 (1 inch) slices.

FRENCH TOAST

1/2 cup flour
1-1/2 tablespoons sugar
1/4 teaspoon grated lemon peel
2 cups milk
6 eggs
18 slices day old bread
1 tablespoon margarine

Beat flour, sugar, lemon peel, milk and eggs until smooth. Soak bread in batter until saturated. Heat margarine in skillet. Cook over medium heat 10 minutes on each side or until golden brown. Sift powdered sugar over the top. Serve with butter and syrup, jam or Raisin Topping.

Makes 18 slices.

According to the Grapevine this is "TOPS"!

RAISIN TOPPING

2/3 cup raisins
1/2 cup honey
1/4 cup margarine
1 teaspoon grated lemon peel

Cover raisins with boiling water and let stand 5 minutes. Drain, cool and chop raisins. Combine with remaining ingredients. Beat with a fork until well blended. Serve over French Toast or waffles.

Makes about 1-1/3 cups.

GERMAN PANCAKES

2 eggs, separated
1-1/2 cups milk
1/2 teaspoon grated lemon peel
1-3/4 cups sugar
1 cup flour, sifted
2 teaspoons baking powder
3/4 cup margarine
7 tablespoons lemon juice

Place egg yolks, milk, lemon peel, 1-1/2 tablespoons sugar, flour, and baking powder in blender. Blend 30 seconds then scrape down sides. Add 1-1/2 tablespoons melted margarine and 2 teaspoons lemon juice. Blend X Refrigerate, covered, 1/2 hour.

Beat egg whites until stiff and fold into batter. Lightly margarine crepe pan or grill. Cook on medium heat. Spoon 1/4 cup batter into hot pan, tilting pan in all directions to coat bottom evenly. Cook until pancakes are brown on bottom, about 30 seconds. Turn over and cook other side about 10 seconds. Flip pancakes over and out onto paper towels. Continue until all batter is used, placing paper towel between each pancake.

In small bowl combine 1/2 cup margarine with 1-1/2 cups sugar and 6 tablespoons lemon juice. Beat until smooth. Spoon about 2 teaspoons mixture on one side of each pancake. Roll up pancake. Transfer to heat proof platter. Continue until all pancakes are rolled up. Drizzle remaining filling over tops. Bake at 500 degrees 5 minutes before serving. Filled crepes may be frozen and reheated at 400 degrees for 15 minutes.

Makes 12 to 14 pancakes.

OVERNIGHT BATTER FOR WAFFLES OR PANCAKES

1 package active dry yeast
5 cups flour
1/3 cup sugar
2 teaspoons soda
1 quart buttermilk
2 tablespoons lemon juice
4 eggs
3/4 cup melted margarine
3/4 cup finely chopped nuts (optional)

In a large bowl, stir together yeast, flour, sugar, soda, and milk. Mix with lemon juice and melted margarine. Beat eggs into batter until blended but lumpy. Stir in nuts. Cover bowl: let rise in a warm place until bubbly(about 30 minutes) or keep in refrigerator overnight.

Bake batter in a preheated waffle baker. Place waffles as they are baked in a single layer directly on the racks in a 300 degree oven for at least 5 minutes.

Or, cool waffles completely on racks. Wrap and freeze for up to one month. Reheat (without thawing) in a toaster.

Makes 6 large or 12 medium waffles.

SHROVE TUESDAY PANCAKES
(First Tuesday in Lent
English Tradition)

Bake pancakes on hot greased griddle. Griddle is hot when a few drops of water dance on surface. Turn pancakes when holes appear on top.

Sprinkle with sugar. Serve on warm plates with lemons to squeeze on top.

Makes 40 pancakes.

ABELSKIVERS

2-1/2 cups flour
1-1/4 teaspoon soda
3/4 teaspoon baking powder
2 cups milk
2 tablespoons lemon juice
2 eggs, separated
3 tablespoons melted margarine

Sift dry ingredients. Beat egg yolks. Add to milk and lemon juice. Combine with dry ingredients. Add melted margarine. Fold in beaten egg whites. Fry in Abelskiver pan. Use knitting needles to turn. Serve with raspberry jam and powdered sugar.

Makes 28 Abelskivers.

FATHER'S DAY BREAKFAST

Cantaloupe Star
*Lemon Poached Fish
*Remoulade Cajun Sauce
*Abelskivers or Waffles
*Raspberry Jam and Powdered Sugar
Strawberries and Whip Cream
Non Fat Milk   Coffee

PIROSHKI

1/2 pound ground beef
1/2 cup minced onion
1/2 cup chopped mushrooms
2 tablespoons lemon juice
1 package refrigerated buttermilk
  biscuits
1 tablespoon margarine, melted

Mix ground beef, onion, mushrooms, and lemon juice. Separate biscuits, cut in halves, and shape into balls. Roll each on floured board to a 3-inch circle. Place a tablespoonful of meat mixture on center of each. Moisten edges and pinch together with a fork over filling; shaping into half-moons. Arrange on ungreased baking sheet and brush with margarine. Bake at 400 degrees for 10 minutes or until brown.

Makes 20 piroshkis.

COTTAGE CHEESE PANCAKES

1 cup cottage cheese
1 tablespoon lemon juice
2 eggs
1/2 cup sifted flour
1/2 teaspoon baking soda

Put all ingredients into blender container and process until smooth. Let stand 10 minutes. Bake on a prepared, moderately hot griddle until brown.

Makes 10 pancakes.

LEMON GLAZED APRICOT-CHEESE BUNS

1 loaf (1 pound) frozen white bread
   dough, thawed, room temperature
1 package (8 ounces) cream cheese
1 egg
1/2 cup snipped dried apricots
   (about 18 halves)

LEMON GLAZE
1 cup powdered sugar
1 tablespoon lemon juice

With floured rolling pin on lightly floured surface, roll dough into an 18 x 12 inch rectangle. Beat cream cheese and egg until blended. Fold in apricots. Spread on dough to within 1 inch of edges. Roll up tightly from one long side. Pinch seam to seal. With very sharp knife, cut in 1 inch slices. Arrange 1 inch apart in single layer in greased 13 x 9 inch baking pan. Cover. Let rise in warm place 40 minutes or until almost doubled. Bake in center of preheated 350 degree oven 30 minutes or until lightly browned. Meanwhile, mix 1 cup powdered sugar and 1 tablespoon lemon juice. Drizzle this over buns while still hot. Serve warm or at room temperature.

Makes 20 buns.

Lemons at room temperature give more juice. Roll first, then cut in half. Press down lightly as you juice. Save shells for garnish by freezing in sealed plastic bags. Label and date the bags!

WALNUT WONDER CAKE

2 cups flour
1 teaspoon baking powder
1 teaspoon soda
1 cup margarine
1 cup sugar
2 eggs
1 cup cottage cheese
1 tablespoon lemon juice
1 teaspoon vanilla

FILLING
1/3 cup packed brown sugar
1/2 cup sugar
1 teaspoon cinnamon
1 cup chopped walnuts

Sift flour, baking powder and soda. Beat margarine and sugar until fluffy. Add 2 eggs and vanilla. Mix with dry ingredients. Blend cottage cheese and lemon juice. Fold in with other ingredients.
Spread half the batter in greased 9X13" pan. Spread half of the filling on top of the batter. Top with the rest of the batter and then the remainder of the filling.

Makes 12 servings.

lemon peel flowers

Pour hot water over citrus. Let stand 5 minutes. Score peel into quarters: remove with fingers. With kitchen shears, cut into tulip or daisy shapes. Let stand in water until ready to use. Attach with toothpicks. Remove picks before serving.

MINCEMEAT COFFEE CAKE

1/2 cup shortening
1 cup sugar
2 eggs
2 cups flour
2 teaspoons baking powder
1 tablespoon lemon juice
7/8 cup milk
1 tablespoon minced lemon peel
1 cup mincemeat
1/2 cup chopped walnuts
2 tablespoons melted margarine
2 tablespoons brown sugar
1 teaspoon cinnamon

Mix shortening and sugar together. Stir in well beaten eggs. Sift flour, measure, then sift again with baking powder. Add lemon juice to milk. Stir into creamed mixture alternately with dry ingredients. Grease and flour a 9 x 13 inch pan. Put half of the dough in the pan.

Combine the lemon peel, mincemeat and nuts. Spread 2/3 of the mincemeat mixture over the batter by the teaspoonful. Cover with remaining batter and dot with rest of mincemeat. Sprinkle with melted margarine, brown sugar, and cinnamon. Bake in a moderate oven (350 degrees) for 45 minutes. Serve hot.

Makes 12 servings.

MINCED LEMON PEEL
Finely chop thin strips of peel to mince.

EGGS BENEDICT

3 English muffins
margarine
6 thin slices ham
6 eggs
1/2 cup Hollandaise sauce

Toast English muffin halves. Spread with margarine while hot. Place ham on each muffin half. Trim to fit muffin. Pile scraps in center. Keep muffins warm while preparing eggs. Poach eggs just until the whites are set, keeping them as round as possible. Put a poached egg on top of the ham on each muffin half and top with Hollandaise Sauce.

Makes 6 servings.

BREAKFAST IN YOSEMITE

*Eggs Benedict
*A for Asparagus
*Grapefruit Star with a Strawberry
*Monkey Bread
Milk and Coffee

Quiet A Baby
All the world loves lemons! When everything else fails a baby will stop crying if given a lemon to suck on.
Parent Ed. tip from For Kid's Sake Organization

HOLLANDAISE SAUCE

2 tablespoons margarine
2 tablespoons flour
1 cup milk
1/8 teaspoon pepper
2 egg yolks
2 tablespoons margarine
3 tablespoons fresh lemon juice

Melt 2 tablespoons margarine over low heat. Blend in flour and cook. Stir constantly until mixture is smooth and bubbly. Remove from heat. Add milk and mix thoroughly. Return to heat. Bring to boil for 1 minute. Keep stirring. Cook until thickened. Remove from heat. Beat in pepper and 2 egg yolks. Gradually add melted margarine and lemon juice. Serve at once or keep warm in a thermos that has been rinsed with very hot water.

Makes 1/2 cup sauce.

*GRAPEFRUIT STAR

Insert knife diagonally in the middle of a grapefruit. Continue around grapefruit in a zigzag pattern, making certain to cut completely through center. Using both hands, twist slightly to pull fruit apart. Decorate with a strawberry in the center.

LEMON POPPY SEED MINIATURE MUFFINS

1 stick (1/2 cup) margarine
4 envelopes Equal, sugar substitute
   each as sweet as 2 teaspoons sugar
2 eggs, separated
2 teaspoons freshly grated lemon peel
1 teaspoon lemon flavoring
1-1/3 cups flour
1 teaspoon baking powder
1/2 teaspoon baking soda
1/2 cup milk
2 teaspoons lemon juice
2-1/2 tablespoons poppy seeds

Beat egg whites until they hold soft peaks. Set aside. Beat margarine, Equal and egg yolks until light. Fold in lemon peel and flavoring. Sift together flour, baking powder and baking soda. Add to the egg mixture alternately with milk and lemon juice. Blend until just combined. Fold in poppy seeds and egg whites. Spoon the batter into miniature muffin pans lined with little paper baking cups. Fill them three fourths full. Bake the muffins in 350 degree oven for 15 minutes or until they spring back to the touch.

Makes 36 muffins.

DIET SPECIAL

*Grapefruit Star
Hard Boiled Egg
*Lemon Poppy Seed Miniature Muffins
Non Fat Milk

ICE BERG BRAN MUFFINS

2 cups boiling water
2 cups 100% Bran
1-1/2 cups margarine
2 cups sugar
1/2 cup molasses
4 eggs
6 cups flour
5 teaspoons soda
1 quart milk
1/4 cup + 1/4 cup lemon juice
Sugar cubes
Raisins, optional

Pour water over bran. Combine milk and 1/4 cup lemon juice. Cream margarine, sugar, molasses and eggs. Add bran, milk, lemon juice, soda and flour. Fill paper baking cup lined muffin tins 3/4 full. Bake 15 minutes at 400 degrees. Dip sugar cubes in lemon juice and lightly place one on top of each muffin as it comes out of the oven.

This batter may be kept up to four weeks in refrigerator and used as needed or baked up and frozen.

1/2 cup raisins may be added to each 2 cups of batter before baking, if desired.

Makes 48 muffins.

.....Easy to keep this batter in refrigerator and bake some muffins fresh to take when you visit someone.

cartwheel twists

Cut unpeeled cartwheel just to center and twist.

LEMON BISCUITS

2 cups biscuit mix
1 cup (1/2 pint) whipping cream
1 tablespoon grated lemon peel
12 sugar cubes
1/2 cup lemon juice

Mix and knead biscuit mix, whipping cream, grated lemon peel. Cut with 2 inch biscuit cutter, dipping in flour and cutting dough.
Dip 12-16 sugar cubes in lemon juice. Press in top of each biscuit. Place cut biscuits, touching each other on all sides, on lightly greased baking sheet. Bake at 450 degrees for 10 minutes.

Makes 12 biscuits.

LEMON HERB SPREAD

1/4 pound soft margarine
2 teaspoons lemon juice
1-1/2 tablespoons snipped parsley or
1 tablespoon freshly minced herbs or
1 teaspoon dried herbs

Mix margarine, lemon juice and herbs. Put in an attractive dish with a curl on top.

Makes 1/2 cup.

Curls
Peel half of fruit away from cartwheel, leaving peel. Curl peel.

FRENCH LEMON PUFFS

1 egg
2 tablespoons sugar
1 lemon, thin peel
1 cup milk
2 cups biscuit mix

TOPPING
1/3 cup margarine, melted
1/2 cup lemon sugar

Heat oven to 400 degrees. Line muffin pans with paper baking cups. Put egg, sugar, peel and milk into blender. Cover and process until peel is chopped fine. Add biscuit mix, continue processing only until mixture is smooth.

Fill muffin pans 1/2 full. Bake 12 minutes or until browned. While muffins are hot, dip into melted margarine and lemon sugar.

Makes 18 puffs.

LEMON SUGAR

3 tablespoons sugar
1/4 teaspoon grated lemon peel

Mix sugar and lemon peel. Store in covered glass jar. Use on cereal, tea, top of muffins, puffs or wherever you need sugar. Nice to give as a small gift in a pretty jar. Include label and uses!

LEMON SUGAR CUBES

Rub all six sides of sugar cube over lemon peel. Store cubes in a jar. It is well worth the time to take to do this.

Main Dishes

ARCADIA CURRY

1 package (12 ounces) frozen shrimp
   or 2 cups chicken or turkey
1 tablespoon margarine
1-1/2 teaspoons curry powder
1 medium tomato
1 medium onion
3 tablespoons lemon juice
1 cup sour cream
4 avocados

Cook shrimp as package directs. Shell and remove black vein. In a saucepan melt margarine with curry. Add chopped tomato and onion. Cook until soft. Add lemon juice, shrimp and sour cream. Heat thoroughly. Cut avocados in halves. Remove avocado seeds and peel. Fill the centers with the hot curry.

Serve with any or all of the following for toppings: Seedless grapes, cherry tomatoes, sliced cucumber, chopped mild onion, shredded coconut, toasted almonds, chutney and raisins.

Makes 8 servings.

LEMON WATER BATH
1/4 cup lemon juice
1 cup water
Mix lemon juice and water. Use to cover peeled and seeded avocados prepared ahead of time. A lemon water bath will keep them from turning brown.

"You Are What You Absorb
Vitamin C improves the absorption of iron from food so the presence or absence of vitamin C can influence the availability of iron greatly."
Len Mervyn, Ph.D. __Minerals and Your Health__

PEACOCK PIE

1 (12 ounce) package stuffing mix
3 cups cubed cooked turkey
1/2 cup margarine
1/2 cup flour
4 cups turkey broth
6 eggs, beaten

Prepare stuffing according to package directions. Spread stuffing in a 13 x 9 inch baking dish. Top with a layer of turkey. Melt margarine. Blend in flour and seasonings. Add broth. Cook and stir until mixture thickens. Stir a small amount of hot mixture into eggs. Return to hot mixture. Pour over turkey. Bake in slow oven (325 degrees) 40 to 45 minutes or until knife inserted to center comes out clean. Let stand 5 minutes to set. Cut in squares. Serve with Red Dot Mushroom Sauce and a sprig of parsley.

RED DOT MUSHROOM SAUCE

1 can mushroom soup
1/4 cup milk
1 cup cottage cheese
1 tablespoon lemon juice
1/4 cup pimiento or canned red pepper.

Blend ingredients in blender. Heat until hot.

Makes 12 servings.

fans or quarter cartwheels

TURKEY MARCO POLO

1-1/2 pounds broccoli
6 thin slices cooked turkey
6 thin slices cooked ham
Mornay Sauce*

Steam broccoli over boiling water until tender. Arrange in 6 individual casseroles or 1-9 x 13" baking dish. Cover with thin slices of turkey and then with ham slices. Spoon Mornay Sauce over ham. Bake at 450 degrees until golden, about 30 minutes.

Makes 6 servings.

MORNAY SAUCE

2 tablespoons margarine, melted
2 tablespoons flour
1 cup milk
1/2 cup margarine, melted
2 egg yolks, beaten
1 tablespoon lemon juice
1/8 teaspoon pepper
3 tablespoons grated Parmesan cheese

Melt 2 tablespoons margarine in saucepan. Stir in flour and cook for 2 or 3 minutes. Do not allow flour to brown. Add milk all at once and continue to cook and to stir until sauce becomes smooth and slightly thickened. Add 1/2 cup melted margarine, beaten egg yolks, lemon juice, pepper and cheese. Heat and stir well.

Makes 1 cup.

PICNIC GAME HENS

8 Cornish hens
1/2 cup Dijon style mustard
2/3 cup white bread crumbs
3 tablespoons minced shallots
1-1/2 cups lemon juice
1/2 cup margarine

Rub each bird with mustard. Sprinkle with bread crumbs. Place in square of foil and fold to center. Add 1 teaspoon shallots, 1 tablespoon margarine and 3 tablespoons lemon juice to each package. Fold foil tightly and bake at 400 degrees for 45 minutes. Open foil, baste and bake approximately 15 minutes more, until browned. Reseal and take to picnic hot or cold. On a picnic keep hot things **HOT** and cold things **COLD** to avoid a disaster.

Makes 8 servings.

HOLLYWOOD BOWL PICNIC
New Twist Sparkling Cider
in champagne glasses
Veggies
Picnic Game Hens
Croissants
Lemon carrots, cold
Wendy's Petite Cherry Cheese Cakes
Box of See's Candy
Silk Rose
Candle Light

CHICKEN DIVAN

1 pound broccoli
1/2 cup mayonnaise
4 tablespoons flour
2 tablespoons lemon juice
1-1/2 cups milk
1-1/2 cups (6 ounces) shredded cheddar
    cheese
2 chicken breasts, cooked, skinned,
    boned, sliced
1/2 cup grated parmesan cheese

Cook broccoli until crisp-tender.
Combine mayonnaise and flour, Gradually
add lemon juice and milk. Cook, stirring
constantly, over low heat until
thickened. Add cheddar cheese. Stir until
melted. Layer broccoli, chicken and sauce
in 11 x 8 inch baking dish. Bake at 350
degrees for 25 minutes. Sprinkle with
parmesan cheese.

Makes 4 servings.

COMPANY DINNER

Bouillon Sipper
Chicken Divan
Steamed Green Beans
Glazed Carrots and Onions
Cranberry Ribbon Loaf Salad
Lemon Biscuits
Mary's Frozen Lemonade Whip

CHICKEN-WALNUT

2 whole chicken breasts
3 tablespoons oil
1 onion , chopped
2 medium stalks celery, chopped
1 tablespoon margarine
3/4 cup coarsely broken walnuts
1 teaspoon finely chopped lemon peel
1 tablespoon fresh lemon juice
2 tablespoons soy sauce

Bone and skin the chicken breasts and cut them into bite-sized pieces. Heat the oil in a skillet over moderate heat until sizzling hot. Add the chicken, green onion and celery. Stir quickly until chicken begins to brown. Add the margarine, nuts and lemon peel. Continue to cook, uncovered, for only a few minutes. Stir often. Turn off the heat. Add soy sauce and lemon juice. Stir until the chicken is well coated with sauce. Serve at once with rice.

Makes 4 servings.

THE LARGEST LEMON*
Mrs. D.G. Knutzen of Whittier, CA reported in May, 1984 a lemon with a circumference of 29-1/2 inches and weighing 8-1/2 pounds.

*Guinness Book of World Records, 1987

WENDY'S GINGER CHICKEN

4 chicken legs (thighs and drumsticks,
  skinned and washed)
  Or 1 chicken cut into 8 serving
  pieces, skinned and washed
3 cloves garlic crushed
1 cup lemon juice
1/2 teaspoon grated lemon peel
1 tablespoon ginger, peeled, chopped
1 cup flour
2 teaspoons paprika
1 teaspoon pepper
2 cups corn oil
1/4 cup chicken broth
1/4 cup brown sugar
2 lemons sliced paper-thin
1 bunch parsley

Marinate chicken for two hours or more in garlic, lemon juice, lemon peel and ginger. Reserve marinade. Put chicken, flour, paprika and pepper in paper bag. Shake. Heat oil in a frying pan. Fry chicken until crispy for 5 to 7 minutes. Place in shallow baking pan. Pour chicken broth and reserved marinade over chicken. Sprinkle with brown sugar. Pat slightly. Arrange lemon slices on top. Bake uncovered 45 minutes in a 350 degree oven. Baste once after 20 minutes. Serve immediately. Garnish with parsley.

Makes 4 servings.

OVEN FRIED CHICKEN

1 fryer, cut up, skinned and washed
1 teaspoon paprika
1/4 cup soy sauce
1/4 cup lemon juice
1 clove garlic, minced
1/8 teaspoon pepper

Cover fryer with paprika, then soak for two or three hours in soy sauce, lemon juice and minced garlic. Sprinkle with pepper. Bake at 350 degrees for 30 minutes. Finish by broiling for five minutes on each side.

Makes 4 servings.

WARM FINGER TOWELS

Wet wash cloths or small napkins with 1/2 water and 1/2 lemon juice solution. Wring out. Fold or roll and heat in microwave on High for 2 to 3 minutes.

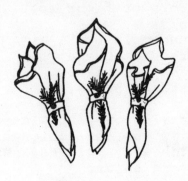

LEMON CHICKEN STIR FRY

2 chicken breasts,skinned, washed
1/2 cup diced red peppers
1 sliced onion
3 sliced yellow (summer) squash
4 tablespoons lemon juice
4 tablespoons water
3 thinly sliced zucchini

Stir fry 2" strips of chicken, red peppers, onion, and yellow squash. Cook with water and lemon juice until chicken is no longer pink. Add zucchini at the very last minute and serve immediately.

Makes 4 servings.

CHICKEN FAJITAS

Lemon Chicken Stir Fry, sizzling hot
12 warm corn or flour tortillas
2 cups salsa
2 cups guacamole (p.91)
1 cup shredded cheese
1/2 cup chopped olives
2 cups refried beans, hot

Put a tortilla on your plate. Fill it as desired with the chicken, salsa, guacamole, cheese, olives and refried beans. Roll and enjoy.

Makes 4 servings.

83

BARBECUED BREAST OF CHICKEN

4 chicken breasts, skinned and washed
1/4 cup lemon juice
1/3 cup Worcestershire sauce

Remove breast bones and flatten out in butterfly style. Pour lemon juice and Worcestershire sauce over chicken. Turn to coat pieces. Allow to marinate about 1 hour or more covered and refrigerated. Cover and microwave on High 16 minutes. Grill 15 minutes over medium heat, turning and basting occasionally with Best Barbecue Sauce. Chicken is done when no longer pink.

Makes 4 servings.

BEST BARBECUE SAUCE

1/2 cup catsup
1 cup bottled barbecue sauce
1 (8 ounce) can tomato sauce
1/4 cup margarine
1/2 cup brown sugar, packed
1 teaspoon cayenne pepper
1/4 teaspoon allspice
1/2 teaspoon instant onion
2 tablespoons lemon juice
1 crushed garlic clove

In 1 quart microwave bowl, combine all of the ingredients and microwave on High, 8 minutes. Stir twice. Refrigerate unused sauce in covered container. Sauce may be used with any meat.

Makes 2-1/2 cups sauce.

CALIFORNIA BAR B Q SPARERIBS

5 pounds country style spareribs
2 lemons, sliced
2 onions, sliced
Best Barbecue Sauce, p.83

Cut ribs into serving pieces. Put the ribs in a shallow roasting pan and top with lemon slices and onion slices. Bake the ribs at 450 degrees for 30 minutes. Drain off fat. Reduce heat to 350 degrees. Pour Best Barbecue Sauce over the ribs. Bake for 30 minutes. When ready to serve, Bar B Q over hot grill for 10 minutes.

Makes 5 servings.

A small wooden crate, purchased in variety or discount stores, can be a "special" container for giving your friends lemons. To make this gift even more appreciated, add little extras. For an extra personal touch add a pretty jar filled with Best Barbecue Sauce or Lemon Sugar. Include a Lemon Twist Cook Book!

MARINATED CHUCK STEAK

4 pound chuck steak, 1-1/2 inches
  thick
1 teaspoon celery seed
1/4 cup finely minced onion
1 clove garlic, minced
1 tablespoon grated lemon peel
1/2 cup lemon juice

Wipe meat with a damp paper towel,
Place in a shallow dish. Combine
remaining ingredients, mixing well. Pour
over meat and refrigerate 12 to 24 hours,
turning meat once or twice. Drain,
reserving marinade. Place meat on broiler
rack 4 to 6 inches from heat. Broil about
8 to 10 minutes on each side for medium
doneness. Or, place on grill over hot
coals: cook 6 to 8 minutes on each side
or until meat is cooked to desired
doneness. Heat drained marinade and serve
with meat.

Makes 8 servings.

MEXICAN MEAL WITH COLOR AND FLAIR

*Lynn's Special Slushy Punch
*6 Layer Acapulco Dip
*Caesar Salad
*Marinated Chuck Steak
*Refried Beans with Cheese
*Lemon Rice
*Mexican Banner Dessert

LEMON VEAL WITH HERBED RICE

1-1/3 cups + 3 tablespoons water
1-1/4 teaspoons chicken bouillon
  granules
1/2 cup rice
2/3 cup coarsely chopped onion
2 garlic cloves, minced
1/2 teaspoon each: basil, oregano
2 veal chops or ground patties,
  4 oz. each, 1/2 inch thick)
1/8 teaspoon allspice
3 tablespoons lemon juice
1/2 lemon, fluted cartwheels
2 teaspoons chopped parsley
Freshly ground pepper, to taste

Bring 1-1/3 cups water and 1 teaspoon of the bouillon granules to a boil. Stir in rice, onion, cloves, basil, and oregano. Cover tightly and simmer 20 minutes. While rice cooks, season veal chops with allspice. Heat over medium heat until hot. Sear chops on both sides. Reduce heat. Add remaining 3 tablespoons water, juice and 1/4 teaspoon bouillon granules. Arrange fluted lemon cartwheels on top of veals. Cover and cook over low heat until tender, about 15 minutes. Remove rice from heat. Let stand covered until all liquid is absorbed, about 5 minutes. Stir in parsley and pepper. Serve with veal. Spoon juices over meat.

Makes 2 servings.

FLUTED LEMON CARTWHEELS
Notch peel with shears or paring knife.

CABBAGE BABIES

1 large head green cabbage
1 large onion
1 pound ground meat
1 cup cooked rice
2 eggs
1 can beef broth
1/4 cup brown sugar
1/4 cup lemon juice
3 tablespoons cornstarch
1 tablespoon prepared horseradish

Cover cabbage in pan of boiling water and turn down to simmer 5 minutes. Carefully remove large leaves from cabbage. Drain and spread out flat. Chop 1/2 cup onion. Slice remainder into 9 X 13 baking dish. Brown the beef. Add onions. Saute until golden brown. Stir in rice and eggs. Divide into 8 portions and place on cabbage leaves. Fold in two sides of each leaf. Roll around meat mixture. Place rolls, seamside down on onions in baking dish. Mix undiluted broth with brown sugar, lemon juice, cornstarch and horseradish. Pour over cabbage rolls. Cover and bake in 400 degree oven for 55 minutes.

Makes 4 servings (2 rolls each).

This wraps up a meal!

88

CHATEAUBRIAND FLAMBE WITH SAVORY STEAK SAUCE

Beef Rib Eye Roast
Coarsely ground black pepper
Lemon extract

Rub pepper onto surface of roast. Place on rack in open pan. Roast in hot oven (400 degrees) for 25 minutes per pound. Remove from oven and let stand 10 to 15 minutes. Place on serving platter. Spoon lemon extract over roast and flame. Slice on diagonal about 1/4 to 1/2 inch thick. Serve with juices from the platter or make Savory Steak Sauce.

Makes 4 servings to the pound with boneless roast.

SAVORY STEAK SAUCE

6 tablespoons margarine, melted
1 clove garlic, pressed
3 tablespoons finely sliced green
  onions
2 teaspoons chopped parsley
1-1/2 teaspoons lemon juice
3 tablespoons Worcestershire sauce
6 fresh mushrooms, sliced.

Cook ingredients 2-3 minutes. Serve over steak.

A sophisticated dish that will impress your guests.

BEEF STROGANOFF

1 pound well trimmed tender beef steak
3 cups sliced fresh mushrooms
3 thinly sliced green onions
6 tablespoons margarine
1/4 teaspoon thyme
1/2 cup water
1/4 cup lemon juice
1 tablespoon cornstarch
3/4 cup canned consomme
1 cup sour cream

Cook mushrooms and onions in 3 tablespoons margarine. Add thyme, lemon juice and water. Simmer until liquid is reduced to 1/4 cup. Add cornstarch mixed with consomme to mushrooms. Cook until mixture boils and thickens. Keep warm. Cut steak into thin, diagonal strips. Brown on both sides in remaining 3 tablespoons margarine. Cook a few strips at a time. Add steak and sour cream to mushroom sauce, heat but do not boil. Sprinkle with chopped parsley. Serve with hot cooked noodles or rice.

Makes 6 servings.

DELUXE DINNER

*Curried Crab Canapes
*Beef Stroganoff over Noodles
*Vegetable Kabobs
*Lemon-Honey Dressing with seasonal fruit
on a grape or fig leaf
*American Lemon Cake with Pour Topping

MEATLOAF WELLINGTON

3/4 cup catsup
1/4 cup brown sugar
3/4 teaspoon dry mustard
1/4 teaspoon allspice
2 tablespoons Worcestershire sauce
dash ground cloves
1-1/2 pounds ground meat
(use at least part ground turkey
to save calories)
3 slices day old bread crumbs
1 egg
1/2 cup lemon juice
1/4 cup chopped onion
8 very thin lemon slices
1 package (8 ounces) refrigerated
   crescent dinner rolls

Mix catsup, sugar, mustard, spices, Worcestershire sauce, meat, bread crumbs, egg, lemon juice and chopped onion. Shape into a 9 x 5 " loaf. Bake in a shallow pan at 350 degrees for 40 minutes. Pour off juices from meatloaf.

Separate crescent roll dough into 4 rectangles. On floured surface arrange with long sides slightly overlapping. Roll out to a 14 x 9" rectangle. Center dough over meatloaf. Fold over edges and tuck under loaf well. Brush with milk and cut a design on top. Place in shallow dish. Bake at 425 degrees for 20 minutes or until golden brown. Serve with thin lemon slices and parsley.

Makes 8 servings.

Beef Wellington: The last 20 minutes of roasting put the crescent roll blanket of dough over a boneless roast. Follow directions above.

GUACAMOLE BURGERS

3/4 cup mashed avocado
3/4 cup chopped tomato
1 tablespoon finely chopped onion
1 small clove garlic, crushed
3 teaspoons lemon juice
1 pound ground beef
4 English muffins, split and toasted

Combine avocado, tomato, onion, garlic, and lemon juice. Set aside. Shape beef into 4 patties. Grill until desired degree of doneness. Place each patty on a muffin half. Top patty with some guacamole mixture and other half of muffin. Serve with chips and remaining guacamole on the side.

Makes 4 servings.

GRADUATION PARTY

*Guacamole Burgers
Chips
*Veggies and Dips
*Carrot Cake with Lemon Cream Frosting
*Lemon Velvet Ice Cream
*Strawberry Sauce
Chocolate Sauce, Nuts, Bananas, and
*Whipped Topping for Do It Yourself
Sundaes
*Pink Lemonade
*Catalina Ice Tea

SWEDISH MEATBALLS
(Microwave)

1 pound ground meat
(use part veal or turkey)
1 small onion, minced
1 clove garlic, crushed
1 tablespoon chopped parsley
2 eggs, beaten
1/4 teaspoon pepper
1/4 teaspoon allspice
1/4 teaspoon nutmeg
1/4 cup bread crumbs
1/4 cup evaporated milk

SAUCE

2 tablespoons flour
1 cup beef broth
1 teaspoon Worcestershire sauce
1 tablespoon lemon juice
1/2 cup creamy cottage cheese
2 tablespoons chopped dill

Combine ingredients for meatballs. Shape into 1 inch balls and place in 1-1/2 quart glass dish. Cover loosely. Microwave on high for 6 minutes. Drain off fat reserving 2 tablespoons. Stir in flour. Add broth slowly. Stir. Add Worcestershire and 1 teaspoon lemon juice. Mix. Pour sauce over meatballs. Cover loosely. Microwave at high 4 minutes. Stir after 2 minutes. Add cottage cheese blended with 2 teaspoons lemon juice and dill. Microwave on medium power 3 minutes or until sauce is bubbly. Serve over hot cooked noodles.

Makes 6 servings.

ROAST RACK OF LAMB

2 racks of 8-rib lamb, all fat removed
  to silver skin
                Marinade
1 onion, chopped
1 clove garlic, minced
1/2 cup wine vinegar
1 cup lemon juice
3 fresh tomatoes,
  finely chopped
4 ounces tomato paste
1 stalk celery, sliced
1 carrot, sliced
1 sprig fresh thyme
1 tablspoon parsley, chopped
1 bay leaf
1 sprig tarragon
1 teaspoon rosemary, chopped
1/8 teaspoon freshly ground pepper

Mix onion, garlic, lemon juice, and vinegar until a liquid consistency in blender. Add all remaining ingredients and stir. Submerge racks of lamb in marinade for 24 hours.

Place lamb in 475 degree oven. Roast for 20 minutes per pound.

When serving, garnish with lemon boats filled with mint jelly.

Makes 1 serving for every two ribs.

Lemon juice is a natural meat tenderizer.

SHISH KABOB

4 pounds leg of lamb
1/4 cup salad oil
1/4 cup lemon juice
2 cloves garlic, minced
1 basket cherry tomatoes
6 bay leaves
2 green peppers, cut in 1" squares
12 pearl onions
1 small eggplant, if desired

Cut meat into 1 inch cubes. Mix oil and lemon juice. Rub into meat. Place in dish. Cover with tomatoes, bay leaves, green peppers, and onions. Refrigerate for 4-5 hours. Sprinkle eggplant with salt. Let stand for 1/2 hour. Then wash, slice and add to dish. Place meat on skewers or spits, alternating with onions, tomatoes, green peppers, eggplant and an occasional bay leaf. Broil on barbeque or in an oven broiler until meat is tender (about 10 minutes on each side). Serve at once with pilaf and salad.

Makes 6 servings.

This mid-eastern entree adapts equally to a formal sit-down dinner or a casual summer gathering on the patio.

LEMON CRANBERRY GLAZED HAM

1 canned ham (2 pound)
1/4 cup firmly packed brown sugar
1 tablespoon cornstarch
1/4 teaspoon ground cloves
1 can (8 ounces) whole berry cranberry
  sauce
1 tablespoon lemon juice
1 teaspoon lemon peel

Combine sugar, cornstarch, cloves, cranberry sauce, lemon juice, and lemon peel in 2 cup glass measure. Stir well and cover loosely. Microwave on High 2 minutes. Stir and set aside. Place ham in a shallow baking dish. Trim excess fat. Cover loosely and microwave on medium power 11 minutes, rotating dish 1/4 turn after 6 minutes. Spoon sauce over ham and microwave on medium power 2 minutes. Let stand 5 to 10 minutes to set glaze. Slice ham and serve with sauce.

Makes 6 servings.

Nice to Know: This is an easy dish to take along on a picnic or potluck because it can be served hot or cold. Slice ham, return to dish, cover and go!

POTLUCK PICNIC
*Lemon Cranberry Glazed Ham
*Finger Food Fruits and *Dip
Blue Cheese with French Bread
*Veggies and *Dill Dip
*Temple City Lemon Bars
*Lemonade with mint

CHERRY WALNUT SAUCE

1 pound can red sour pitted cherries
1 tablespoon cornstarch
1/3 cup sugar
2 tablespoons lemon juice
1/4 cup chopped walnuts

Drain cherries. Save the liquid. In saucepan combine cornstarch and sugar. Stir in cherry liquid and lemon juice until smooth. Add walnuts. Cook over medium heat until thick and clear. Add cherries and bring to a boil. Serve sauce over hot meat or on the side in lemon cups.

Makes 1-1/2 cups sauce.

Wonderful sauce with chicken, turkey or ham.
Vitamin C doubles the absorption of iron when eaten at the same meal.

ORIGIN OF LEMONS

"Lemons probably originated in North East India near the Himalayas. They were taken by the Arabs to the Mediterranean around 100 A.D. and to Europe by the Crusaders about 1000 A.D."
World Book Encyclopedia, 1986

PINEAPPLE SAUCE WITH HAM

1/3 cup canned apricot quarters
1 cup cubed fresh pineapple
1/4 cup nuts
1/4 cup raisins
1/2 cup lemon juice
1/2 cup apricot juice
1 tablespoon cornstarch
2 tablespoons sugar
1/4 teaspoon cinnamon

Combine cornstarch, sugar and cinnamon with a small amount of the apricot juice. Heat lemon and apricot juice. Slowly add cornstarch mixture to hot liquid. Stir constantly until thickened. Add apricots, pineapple, nuts, and raisins. Pour sauce into pineapple bowl. Serve with ham.

Makes 12 servings.

Excellant served with any meat.

PINEAPPLE BOWL

Cut top off 3/4 to 1 inch below leaves on pineapple. Set top aside. To hollow out fruit, cut around outside edge of fruit with a sharp bread knife. Leave a wall 1/2 inch thick so shell will hold it's shape. Be careful not to cut into the sides or bottom of the pineapple shell.

HONG KONG PORK CHOPS

8 loin pork chops
1 onion, thinly sliced
1/4 cup soy sauce
1/4 cup orange juice
1/4 cup lemon juice
1 can (4 ounces) sliced mushrooms,
   undrained
1/2 teaspoon ground ginger
1/4 teaspoon garlic powder
1/2 green pepper, chopped
1/2 can (4 ounces) water chestnuts,
   sliced
1 lemon, unpeeled, sliced into half
   cartwheels

Brown chops on both sides. Drain off excess fat. Cover with onion slices. Combine soy sauce, orange juice, lemon juice, mushrooms, ginger and garlic powder. Pour over chops. Bake covered at 350 degrees for 35 minutes. Add green pepper, water chestnuts and lemon slices. Bake uncovered for 15 minutes longer. Serve with steamed rice.

Makes 8 servings.

The Whole World Wants California Lemons

"During the Cold War break through sales of lemons were made to the East Bloc.
   In 1964 Sunkist paved the way for elimination of Japan's import quota on fresh lemons.
   Sunkist is the largest marketing coop in the world. Headquarters are in Sherman Oaks, California."
Sunkist Growers, Inc.
Charles F. Queenan

TUNA BOATS

6 hot dog buns
2 (7 ounce cans) tuna
4 hard cooked eggs, diced
2 tablespoons lemon juice
2 tablespoons onion, minced
1 small green pepper, diced
2 tablespoons pickle relish
4 tablespoons mayonnaise

Split hot dog buns. Combine remaining ingredients. Spoon into buns. Wrap in foil. Bake in 300 degree oven for 30 minutes. Put a paper triangle on a skewer and stick in bun to serve as a "boat". While adults are having tea, put a blue sheet on the floor in another room and serve these to children picnic style.

Makes 6 servings.

HIGH TEA PARTY

*Crisp Cucumber Slices in Mock Champagne
*Date Nut Bread with Cream Cheese
Sandwiches
*Pineapple Lemon Loaf with Cream Cheese
Sandwiches
*Myrna's Lemon Bread
*Tom Thumb Lemon Tarts
*Lemon Fruit Slices
*Angel Whispers
*Fruit Sorbet
*Fresh Strawberries
*Perfect Cuppa Tea

Vitamin C in your body doesn't stay
So be sure to have some lemon everyday!

SANDWICH IN THE ROUND

12 ounces thinly sliced cooked meat
  (turkey, chicken, ham, or beef)
1/2 cup mayonnaise
1 tablespoon spicy mustard
1 teaspoon lemon juice
1/2 teaspoon Worcestershire sauce
1 round (1 pound) loaf rye bread
1 cup coarsely chopped Romaine lettuce
3/4 cup shredded Cheddar cheese
1 medium tomato, thinly sliced

Combine mayonnaise, mustard, lemon juice and Worcestershire sauce. Using long bread knife, slice off top 2 inches of loaf. Remove center portion of bread, leaving a shell approximately 1 inch thick. To assemble, layer ingredients in the following order in the loaf: lettuce, 1/3 of the meat, 1/2 of the cheese and 1/2 of the tomato slices, repeat layers, ending with a meat layer. Spread with mayonnaise, mustard and lemon juice mixture or serve it on the side. Replace bread top. Wrap and refrigerate until ready to serve. Put a long sandwich pick in six intervals. Cut into 6 wedges.

Makes 6 servings.

Grow and Enjoy a Lemon Tree
Lemons can be grown indoors in containers, or outdoors in temperate climates.
For more information look for:
Citrus, How to Select, Grow and Enjoy, published by HP Books, Inc. P.O.Box 5367, Tucson, AZ 85703

TUNA MELT

1/2 cup margarine
16 slices rye bread
16 slices Swiss Cheese
2 cups Tuna Salad

Lightly spread margarine on one side of bread and place with margarined side down on grill. Place a slice of Swiss cheese on each slice of bread and grill until cheese melts. Spread Tuna Salad on 8 of the bread slices and top with remaining 8 slices to make sandwiches. Remove from griddle and cut diagonally.

Makes 8 sandwiches.

TUNA SALAD

2 (7 ounce) cans tuna, drained
1/2 cup chopped celery
1/4 cup chopped onion
1 tablespoon lemon juice
1/2 cup mayonnaise

Combine drained tuna, celery, onion and lemon juice. Mix well and toss with enough mayonnaise to just moisten tuna mixture. Tomatoes stuffed with Tuna Salad are great, too!

Makes 2 cups.

Lemon will enhance but never disguise fish and seafood.

TUNA CASSEROLE

2 eggs
2 cups cottage cheese
1 (7 ounce) can tuna
1 teaspoon lemon juice
1/4 cup soft bread crumbs
1 cup frozen peas
1/2 cup buttered bread crumbs or
    crumbled potato chips

In a 1 quart casserole blend all ingredients except buttered bread crumbs. Top with crumbs or chips. Bake at 350 degrees for 30 minutes or until just set.

Makes 4 servings.

Serve with a Smile

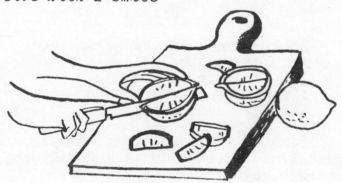

LEMON WEDGE or SMILE

For extra seasoning and more eye appeal serve with a lemon wedge on the side.
To make it easier to hold when squeezing cut off each end of the lemon wedge or smile.

COQUILLES SAINT-JACQUES

3 green onions, chopped fine
  (greens,too)
4 tablespoons margarine (total)
4 ounces fresh mushrooms, chopped
1 can (10-1/2 ounces) cream of chicken
  soup
1/2 cup lemon juice
White pepper to taste
1 tablespoon parsley, chopped fine
2 cans (7 ounces) tuna, drained
2 tablespoons Parmesan cheese
1 slice bread, crusts removed
6 lemon smiles dipped in paprika
6 sea shells, rubbed with margarine

Cook onions in 2 tablespoons margarine until tender. Remove from heat. Brown mushrooms quickly in 1 tablespoon margarine. Combine soup and lemon juice. Heat to boiling. Season to taste. Mix half of sauce with onions and mushrooms. Spoon equally into 6 margarined sea shells. Add parsley and tuna. Top with remainder of sauce. Combine bread and cheese in blender. Sprinkle over sauce. Drizzle 1 tablespoon melted margarine over crumbs. Heat in 350 degree oven 10 minutes or until browned. Serve hot with lemon smiles dipped in paprika.

Makes 6 servings.

wedges or smiles

BARBECUED SALMON

1 (5 to 8 pound) whole dressed
   fresh/frozen salmon, thawed
2 tablespoons margarine, softened
1/2 medium onion, sliced
1/2 lemon, sliced
1/4 cup parsley
1/4 cup oil
12 lemon wedges

Wash salmon and pat dry. Sprinkle inside of salmon with pepper. Dot with margarine. Arrange overlapping slices of onion, lemon and parsley in cavity. Brush salmon with oil. Wrap in heavy-duty aluminum foil. Seal edges with double fold. Place on grill over medium hot coals. Carefully turn salmon every 10 minutes. Test for doneness after 45 minutes by inserting meat thermometer in thickest part. Cook to internal temperature of 160 degrees or until salmon flakes easily when tested with a fork at thickest part. To serve, transfer salmon to serving platter and fold back foil. Cut between bone and meat with a wide spatula. Lift off each serving. Serve with lemon wedges and parsley.

Makes 8 to 12 servings.

Wedges

Cut lemons lengthwise into 6 or 8 wedges. Decorate with red pepper or parsley.

BROILED SALMON WITH HERBED LEMON

8 (about 4 ounces each) fresh or
    frozen salmon fillets
1/4 cup margarine, melted
2 tablespoons lemon juice
2 tablespoons chopped parsley
1/4 teaspoon dill weed, rosemary or
    marjoram, crushed
1/4 teaspoon coarsely ground pepper

Line broiler pan with foil and place
salmon fillets on the well-greased rack.
Combine remaining ingredients. Baste
salmon with mixture. Broil 4 inches from
heat allowing 10 minutes cooking time per
inch of thickness measured at thickest
part or until salmon flakes easily when
tested with a fork. Do not turn salmon.
Baste several times during broiling.
Serve with lemons to squeeze.

Makes 8 servings.

Lemon to Squeeze

Cut lemons crosswise in half. Wrap
lemon halves in yellow cheese cloth
circles and tie with green ribbon. When
you squeeze the cheese cloth strains out
the seeds.

SHRIMP LORRAINE

1-1/2 cups sliced celery
1 cup chopped onions
1 (8 ounces) can sliced mushrooms,
   drained
2 tablespoons margarine
1 can cream of shrimp soup
2 tablespoons lemon juice
1/4 teaspoon pepper
1/4 teaspoon tarragon
1 (8 ounces) package frozen, peeled
   cooked shrimp
1/2 cup sour cream
1 tablespoon chopped parsley
3 cups hot cooked rice

Cook celery, onions and mushrooms in margarine until tender.

Stir in soup, lemon juice, pepper, tarragon and shrimp. Just before serving add sour cream and parsley and heat through. Do not boil. Serve over rice.

Makes 6 servings.

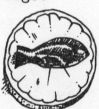

Pimiento
cut-outs

Cleaning Copper and Aluminum

Use lemons and salt for cleaning copper and aluminum.

SALMON LOAF

2 eggs
2/3 cup milk
1 tablespoon lemon juice
3/4 cup bread crumbs
2 tablespoons margarine
1 (16 ounces) can salmon
1 tablespoon paprika
6 lemon stars

Put eggs and milk in mixing a bowl and beat with fork until blended. Add lemon juice and crumbs. Melt margarine in microwave. Use margarine wrapper to grease sides of pie pan. Pour melted margarine into mixture in bowl. Add salmon with the liquid and flake with fork. Mix well and spread in pie pan. Bake 35 minutes, or until firm. Cut in wedges and serve warm with lemon stars dipped in paprika.

Makes 6 servings.

LEMON STARS

Cut into the middle of a lemon with sharp knife. Make "V" cuts all the way around the outside. Be sure to connect each new cut with the last cut made. Keep the zigzag line as straight as possible. When the zigzag line is complete and you come around to where you started, the lemon will come apart easily leaving a nice "star". Cut a small slice off the bottom so that it will not tip over. Dip it in paprika, if desired.

BETTY'S CRABMEAT LUNCHEON DISH

2 (6 ounces) frozen crabmeat, thawed
1 (8 ounces) package cream cheese
3 tablespoons mayonnaise
2 tablespoons onion, chopped
3 teaspoons lemon juice
1/8 teaspoon Worcestershire sauce
1/8 teaspoon Tabasco
8 Holland rusks or toasted English
  Muffins
2 large ripe tomatoes, sliced
8 slices American processed cheese

The night before serving, mix together the crabmeat, cheese, mayonnaise, and seasonings. Refrigerate. To prepare for serving, margarine rusks slightly. Divide crab mixture evenly on top of rusks. Cover each with cheese slice. Top with slice of tomato. Bake in 350 degree oven until mixture is hot (25 to 30 minutes).

Makes 8 servings.

Imitation crabmeat is just as good.

LUNCHEON ON THE TERRACE

Betty's Crabmeat Luncheon Dish
Asparagus
Slice of cantaloupe and honeydew melon
Lemon Cloud Pie
Perfect Cuppa Tea

fancy cartwheels

SHRIMPS IN LOBSTER SAUCE

2 tablespoons peanut oil
2 cloves garlic, crushed
1/4 pound ground pork
1 pound uncooked shrimps, shelled and
   deveined
1 tablespoon soy sauce
1/2 teaspoon sugar
4 teaspoons lemon juice
2 green onions cut in 2" pieces
1/4 cup water
1 tablespoon cornstarch dissolved in 1
   tablespoon water
2 eggs, slightly beaten

Heat oil in skillet. Stir in garlic. Add pork and continue stirring until the meat turns white, about 3 minutes. Add shrimps. Stir until they turn pink. Add next five ingredients. Mix well. Cover and bring to boil. Turn to simmer and cook for 3 minutes. Add cornstarch mixture to sauce. Stir until thickened. Quickly blend in slightly beaten eggs. Take off burner. Serve immediately.

Makes 4 servings.

Chinese call this "lobster sauce". It doesn't contain any lobster. They call it "lobster sauce" because it is one of the sauces used with lobster. It is delicious served very hot with boiled rice.

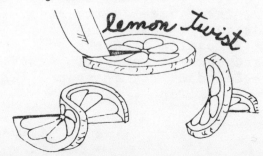

lemon twist

LEMON POACHED FISH

1 pound fresh Halibut (or any fish)
1 tablespoon fresh lemon juice

Cut fish into individual sized servings. Put enough water in a pan to barely cover fish. Add lemon juice. Bring to a boil. Place the fish in the water. Cover and cook below boiling point for 8 to 10 minutes. Carefully remove fish from water and serve immediately with Hollandaise Sauce and lemon smiles.

Makes 4 servings.

WHEN THE DISH IS FISH

Baking fish on a bed of chopped onion, celery and parsley not only makes fish taste better, but also keeps it from sticking to the pan.

Thaw frozen fish in milk. The milk draws out the frozen taste and provides the fresh-caught flavor.

After preparing fish rub your cutting boards and counter tops with lemon. Drop lemon shells down the disposal. This will freshen your kitchen.

REMOULADE CAJUN SAUCE

2 eggs, soft boiled
1/4 teaspoon pepper
1/2 teaspoon dried mustard
1 clove garlic
1 teaspoon dill weed
1 small sweet pickle
1-1/2 tablespoons lemon juice
1 cup oil
2 tablespoons capers
1 or 2 drops tabasco
1 hard cooked egg, quartered and chopped

Put eggs, seasonings, pickle, and lemon juice into blender. Process a few seconds. Remove feeder cap. Pour in oil in a steady stream until mixture is thick. Fold in capers, tabasco, and chopped egg. Serve with shrimp and other fish.

Makes 1-1/2 cups.

CAJUN MAYONNAISE

1 cup mayonnaise
1/4 teaspoon tabasco sauce
1/4 cup lemon juice

Blend all ingredients until smooth. Chill. Serve with hot vegetables or salads.

Makes 1 cup.

Variations:
Curry: Blend in 1 tablespoon curry.
Pink: Blend in 2 tablespoons ketchup.

Salads

AVOCADO RING

1 (3 ounce) package lime gelatin
1 cup hot water
3 tablespoons minced parsley
1 cup mashed avocado
3/4 cup cream cheese
3/4 cup mayonnaise
1 teaspoon lemon juice

Dissolve gelatin in hot water. Chill until it begins to congeal. Fold in remaining ingredients. Fill oiled ring mold. Chill until firm. Surround with fresh fruit. Serve with Creamy Lemon Dressing.

Makes 6 servings.

CREAMY LEMON DRESSING

1/3 cup frozen lemonade concentrate
1/3 cup honey
1/3 cup sour cream
1 teaspoon celery seed

Mix all ingredients in blender.

Makes 3/4 cup.

SUBSTITUTE SOUR CREAM
1/3 cup creamy cottage cheese and 1 teaspoon lemon juice. Blend well.
This can be doubled or tripled.

CAESAR SALAD

1 clove garlic, crushed
2/3 cup olive oil
4 quarts romaine (3 medium heads)
1/8 teaspoon pepper
1 tablespoon Worcestershire sauce
1 soft boiled egg
4 tablespoons lemon juice
2 tablespoons wine vinegar
6 anchovy fillets, chopped
1/2 cup Parmesan cheese
1 cup croutons

Add garlic to oil. Let stand overnight. Discard garlic. Place romaine, washed, chilled and torn in large salad bowl. Sprinkle with pepper and Worcestershire sauce. Put soft boiled egg into middle of salad. Pour lemon juice and vinegar over egg. Toss lightly to mix well. Add remaining ingredients, tossing after each addition.

Makes 12 servings.

This is a great salad to build and toss in front of guests. It originated in Tijuana, Mexico.

GREEN AND GOLD SALAD

1 envelope unflavored gelatin
1 cup orange juice
3 tablespoons lemon juice
1 can (8 ounces) pineapple chunks
1 cup coarsely grated raw carrot
1/4 cup sugar

Drain liquid from pineapple into 2 cup measure. Add orange juice to make 1-1/2 cups. Pour 1/2 cup of mixture into saucepan. Sprinkle gelatin over liquid. Place over low heat. Stir constantly until gelatin dissolves, 2 to 3 minutes. Remove from heat. Stir in remaining liquid, sugar and lemon juice. Add pineapple and grated carrot. Turn into 3-cup mold (6" dish). Chill until firm. Unmold. Garnish with salad greens and lemon twists.

Makes 4 servings.

For 12 servings: triple the recipe and use a 9"x13" pan. Put 2 drops of yellow food coloring in 1 cup mayonnaise. Spread on top. It is ready to go to a picnic or a potluck.

Lemons have many uses. In addition to health, flavor and eye appeal in foods they can be used as a perfume or as a bleach.

LEMON PINEAPPLE CHEESE JELLO

2 (3 ounce) packages lemon jello
1 (8 ounce) pkg. processed cheese
1 (8 ounce) can crushed pineapple
1 (3 ounce) package of cream cheese
4 cups Whipped Topping

Cut processed cheese into tiny chunks. Dissolve jello in two cups very hot water. Beat cream cheese with one cup liquid (pineapple juice + water). Fold in crushed pineapple and processed cheese. Chill until syrup. Fold in Whipped Topping. Chill until firm.

Makes 8 servings.

WHIPPED TOPPING

3/4 cup nonfat dry milk powder
3/4 cup ice water
6 envelopes Equal (each as sweet as 2
    teaspoons sugar)
3 teaspoons lemon juice

Whip dry milk powder with ice water until soft peaks form(about 3 to 4 minutes). Add lemon juice. Beat until stiff. Sweeten with Equal.

Makes 4 cups.

LEMON BOATS OR CUPS

Cut lemons in half. Squeeze out juice. Freeze juice in ice cube tray. Scrape out pulp. Fill lemon "boats" with jello. Chill until firm.

lemon boats

MACADAMIA CHICKEN SALAD

4 large pineapples
2 cups diced cooked chicken
1 cup sliced celery
2 oranges, peeled and cut in segments
2 cups seedless grapes
3 kiwi, peeled and sliced
Any other fruit or berries in season
3/4 cup Miracle Whip
1 teaspoon soy sauce
2 teaspoons lemon juice
1/2 cup chopped macadamia nuts
1/2 cup slivered almonds

Cut a horizontal slice in each pineapple to make a boat. Leave top intact. Remove meat of pineapple. Cut into chunks. In large bowl, combine pineapple, chicken, oranges, grapes, kiwi. Toss with Miracle Whip, soy sauce and lemon juice. Keep refrigerated. Before serving, toss with nuts. Serve in pineapple shells.

Makes 8 servings.

I served this at a wedding reception-----
received many compliments!

J. Webber (1943) listed 21 varieties of lemons. An unusual bearer may produce 7,000 lemons a year.

Encyclopedia Brittanica, 1975

NIPPY BEET SALAD

1 (3 ounce) box raspberry gelatin
1 (8 ounce) can shoestring beets
1 (8 ounce) can crushed pineapple
2 tablespoons lemon juice
1 tablespoon horseradish
3/4 cup chopped celery

Drain the beets. Heat the juice with sufficient water to make 3/4 cup. Stir in gelatin to dissolve. Cool. Drain the pineapple juice. To the drained pineapple juice, add the lemon juice, horseradish, and water to make 1 cup liquid. Add to cooled gelatin mixture. Fold in beets, pineapple and celery. Place in mold. Refrigerate until set. Garnish with a lemon twist.

Makes 4 servings.

Christopher Columbus, Our Hero

In 1492 Columbus discovered America while in search of gold, silk and food for Spain.
"He planted the first lemon trees in America in 1493."
The twist is that Christopher Columbus brought us the food, and it is worth more than gold!

World Book Encyclopedia, 1986

PERFECTION SALAD

1 envelope unflavored gelatin
1/4 cup sugar
1-1/4 cups water, divided
1/4 cup lemon juice
1/2 cup finely shredded cabbage
1 cup shredded carrot
1 pimiento, cut in small pieces

Mix gelatin and sugar in small saucepan. Add 1/2 cup of water. Place over low heat. Stir until gelatin is dissolved. Remove from heat. Stir in remaining 3/4 cup water, lemon juice. Chill to unbeaten egg white consistency. Fold in vegetables. Turn into a 2 cup mold or individual molds. Chill until firm. Unmold. Garnish with salad greens. Serve with mayonnaise thinned with lemon juice.

Makes 4 servings.

To serve 12 triple the recipe and use a 9" x 13" dish.

Try these combinations, too.
Chopped celery, shredded cabbage, chopped pepper or pimiento
Shredded carrot, orange sections, diced canned pineapple
Chopped cucumber and onion
Drained mixed fruits or cooked mixed vegetables.

"The average lemon tree produces 1,500 fruits a year."
Encyclopedia Brittanica, 1975

SALAD SURPRISE

1 pineapple, peeled and diced
2 cups cherry tomatoes, cut in halves
2 medium avocados, peeled and diced
Juice of 1 lemon
1 cup red wine vinegar
1 small clove garlic, minced
1/2 cup oil
1 head lettuce

Combine pineapple, tomatoes, and avocados in large bowl. Combine lemon juice, vinegar, garlic and oil. Pour dressing over pineapple mixture. Toss to mix. Refrigerate for several hours. Drain. Serve in lettuce cups.

Makes 6 servings.

Often requested recipe from the Mauna Kea in Hawaii.

lemon peel flowers see p. 64

CELEBRATION DINNER

*No Sugar and Regular Lemonade
with Mint
*Macadamia Cheese Ball
Crackers
*Chafing Dish Scampi
*Salad Surprise
*Chateaubriand Flambe
*Boiled Artichokes
*Lemon Biscuits
*Fruit Sherbet
*Lemon Layer Coconut Cake
*Coffee Diable

TUNA TABOULLI SALAD

1 cup boiling water
1/4 cup dry cracked wheat (Bulgur)
1 to 2 cans water packed tuna
1 tomato, chopped
1/2 cup parsley, chopped
2 green onions with tops, sliced
1/4 cup lemon juice
1 head Boston lettuce, washed

Pour water over Bulgur in bowl. Let stand 1 hour. Drain. Toss with remaining ingredients. Chill.

Optional ingredients to add: 1/4 cup chopped mint, 2 tablespoons olives, 1/4 cup diced celery, 1/4 cup diced cheese, 1/4 cup cooked vegetables, 1 cup cooked leftover meats.

DILL CUCUMBER SAUCE

1 cup plain unflavored yogurt
1/2 cucumber peeled, seeded, chopped
1/2 teaspoon dill weed
1 tablespoon lemon juice
1/8 teaspoon garlic powder

Combine all ingredients and chill.

To serve, spoon tuna mixture onto center of plates. Serve on lettuce. Serve sauce on the side in a lemon boat.

Makes 4 servings.

Use plenty of lemon juice for a great sharp, sour taste!

CRANBERRY RIBBON LOAF

1 (16 ounce) can whole cranberry sauce
2 tablespoons lemon juice
1/2 pint whipping cream
1/4 cup powdered sugar
2/3 cup chopped nuts
1 (8 ounce) can crushed pineapple

Drain pineapple. Combine cranberry sauce with lemon juice. Pour into loaf pan or refrigerator tray. Whip the cream. Blend together whipped cream, sugar, nuts and pineapple. Layer whipped cream mixture over cranberry sauce. Freeze until firm. Serve in slices as salad or dessert.

Makes 10 servings.

To Make Ahead-
Line the pan with heavy plastic wrap. When salad is solid, remove from pan and wrap tightly with freezer wrap. Date and label to store in freezer.

The First Citrus in California
"The citrus industry in California began in 1804 when Spanish missionaries planted 400 orange seeds at the San Gabriel Mission."
California   Past/Present/Future: Information Almanac, 1975

BLACK CHERRY JELLO WITH LEMON CENTER

1 can dark-sweet, pitted cherries
2 (3 ounce) box raspberry jello
1 (3 ounce) box lemon jello
1 (3 ounce) package cream cheese
1/2 pint whipping cream
1 cup walnuts or pecans

Dissolve raspberry jello with drained cherry juice plus boiling water to equal 4 cups. Add the cherries and nuts. Divide in half. Put one layer in the bottom of a 9 x 13 inch pan to set. Dissolve the lemon jello with 1/2 cup boiling water. Combine 1 cup cold water and ice cubes to make 1-1/2 cups ice and water. Add to gelatin. Stir until slightly thickened. If necessary, remove unmelted ice. Whip the cream. Mix with the cream cheese. Add to lemon jello. Place on the first layer of cherries and jello. When this is soft-set, add the other half of the raspberry jello, cherries and nuts to the top. Chill until firm.

Makes 18 servings.

Special occasion jello salad!

Limeys
A daily serving of lemon or lime juice was prescribed for every member of the British navy to prevent scurvy. That is why their sailors are called "Limeys".

SHRIMP OR CRAB FRUIT SALAD

2 cups torn or shredded lettuce
1 pound crab or shrimp
24 sections pink grapefruit
2 avocados, peeled, halved and sliced to form decorative fan
1 papaya, peeled, quartered and sliced to form decorative fan
4 lemon wedges
Yogurt Sauce*

Arrange lettuce in centers of 4 plates. Place row of alternating crab and grapefruit pieces over lettuce. Arrange 1 avocado fan on one side of each plate and 1 papaya fan on other side. Garnish with lemon. Serve with Yogurt Sauce.

Makes 4 servings.

YOGURT SAUCE

2 cups yogurt
3/4 cup tarragon leaves, coarsely chopped
1/2 cup freshly squeezed lemon juice

Blend yogurt, tarragon and lemon juice. Refrigerate.

Makes 2-1/2 cups.

Serve with "smiles" to squeeze!

CLASSIC WALDORF SALAD

2 cups diced, unpeeled apples
1 tablespoon sugar
1 tablespoon lemon juice
1 cup 1"-pencil thin sliced celery
1/2 cup chopped walnuts
1/4 cup mayonnaise
1 head lettuce, washed

Sprinkle diced apples with sugar and lemon juice. Combine apples, celery and nuts. Gently fold mayonnaise into apple mixture. Chill. Serve in lettuce-lined bowl or as individual servings.

Makes 6 servings.

KNIFE AND COUNTER SAVER
Always use a cutting board when slicing or chopping.

FROZEN FRUIT SALAD

1 package (3 ounce) lemon gelatin
1 cup boiling water
1 can (8-3/4 ounce) pineapple tidbits
1/3 cup mayonnaise
1/4 cup lemon juice
1 cup heavy cream
1 medium banana, diced
1/2 cup seeded halved grapes
1/4 cup diced maraschino cherries
1/4 cup chopped nuts

Dissolve gelatin in boiling water. Drain pineapple. Measure syrup. Add water to make 1/2 cup, if necessary. Stir into gelatin with lemon juice. Blend in mayonnaise. Chill until very thick. Whip the cream. Fold into gelatin with fruits and nuts. Pour into 2 freezing trays or a 9 x 5 inch loaf pan. Freeze until firm (at least 3 to 4 hours). Slice or cut in squares.

Makes 8 servings.

Decorate with a Lemon Twist

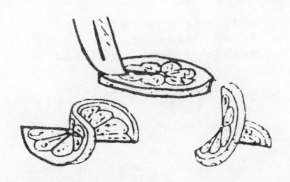

TWENTY FOUR HOUR SALAD

1 (8 ounces) can pineapple tidbits
2 eggs, slightly beaten
1/4 cup sugar
1/4 cup flour
1/2 cup lemon juice
1 cup heavy cream, whipped
16 marshmallows (quartered)
1/2 cup chopped walnuts
1 cup seedless grapes
1/3 cup walnut halves
1 basket strawberries

Drain pineapple, reserving 1/2 cup syrup. In saucepan mix syrup with eggs, sugar, and flour. Cook over low heat, stirring constantly, until very thick and smooth. Stir in lemon juice. Refrigerate until cool. Fold in whipped cream. Lightly mix in pineapple, marshmallows, chopped nuts and grapes. Cover. Refrigerate for 24 hours.

To Serve: Cut in squares or serve in lemon shells. Garnish with walnut halves and strawberries.

Makes 10 servings.

SHOWER PARTY

*Lemon Sherbet Punch
*A No Drink with a Twist
*Frosted Sandwich Loaf
*Veggies
*24 Hour Fruit Salad
*Pink Lemonade Party Pie

CREAMY GARLIC DRESSING

1/3 cup lemon juice
3/4 cup salad oil
2/3 cup evaporated milk
2 cloves garlic
1/2 teaspoon sugar
1/4 teaspoon white pepper
1/2 teaspoon paprika

Put all ingredients into blender container. Cover. Whip until blended. Refrigerate.

Makes 2 cups.

THOUSAND ISLAND DRESSING

2 hard boiled eggs
1 cup mayonnaise
1 tablespoon catsup
1 teaspoon prepared mustard
1 teaspoon fresh grated lemon peel
1 tablespoon lemon juice

Peel and dice hard boiled eggs. Combine remaining ingredients. Fold in eggs. Chill. Serve on Rueben sandwiches, fish sandwiches, or salads.
Makes 1-1/2 cups.

LEMON CUPS
Serve dressing on the side in lemon cups.

BLUE CHEESE DRESSING

3 cups cottage cheese
1-1/2 cups buttermilk
2 tablespoons lemon juice
2 tablespoons minced green onions
2 tablespoons snipped parsley
2 ounces blue cheese, crumbled

Place cottage cheese, buttermilk and lemon juice in blender container. Blend until smooth. If too thick, add more buttermilk. Stir in green onions, blue cheese and parsley.

Makes 1 quart.

SUNDAY NIGHT SUPPER

*Mulligatawny Soup
*Blue Cheese or *Creamy Garlic Dressing
with mixed green salad
French Bread
*Lemon Ice

Serve a "smile" to squeeze for those who don't want salad dressing. Jab a fork into the center of the smile and squeeze over salad.

LIVELY LEMON FRENCH DRESSING

1 teaspoon unflavored gelatin
1 tablespoon cold water
1/4 cup boiling water
1 tablespoon sugar
1 teaspoon grated lemon peel
1/2 cup lemon juice
1 clove garlic, minced
Dash of pepper
1/8 teaspoon dry mustard
1/4 teaspoon Worcestershire

Soften gelatin in cold water. Add boiling water, stirring until thoroughly dissolved. Stir in sugar until dissolved. Combine mixture with remaining ingredients in a container with a tight fitting lid. Shake well. Dressing may be covered and stored in refrigerator until needed. If refrigerated before serving, place container of dressing in pan of hot water for 5 minutes to re-liquefy the gelatin. Serve cool, but not chilled, over crisp salad greens.

Makes 1 cup.

Diet tip: 1 tablespoon Lively Lemon French Dressing = 10 calories.

only 3 calories a squeeze

LEMON-HONEY DRESSING

1/2 cup lemon juice
1/2 cup honey

Mix lemon juice and honey in equal parts.

Makes 1 cup.

Serve a choice of Lemon-Honey or Coconut Dressing with fruit on the half-shell. Fill an avocado half with chilled fresh fruit: melon balls, grapes, pineapple, strawberries, or any other fruit in season. Pass the dressings.

COCONUT DRESSING

1/4 cup light corn syrup
2 tablespoons lemon juice
2/3 cup mayonnaise
1/4 teaspoon ground ginger
1/3 cup grated coconut

Blend together corn syrup, lemon juice and mayonnaise until smooth. Stir in ground ginger and coconut.

Makes 1-1/4 cups.

AVOCADO SALAD DRESSING

1 avocado, halved, pitted and peeled
3 tablespoons lemon juice
2/3 cup evaporated milk
1/4 teaspoon pepper
1/2 medium onion
1/4 teaspoon liquid pepper sauce

Cut avocado into pieces. Place in container of blender. Add remaining ingredients. Cover and blend until dressing is smooth. Chill before serving.

Makes 1-1/3 cups.

orange peel flowers

Pour hot water over citrus. Let stand 5 minutes. Score peel into quarters: remove with fingers. With kitchen shears, cut into tulip or daisy shapes. Let stand in water until ready to use. Attach with toothpicks. Remove picks before serving.

EQUIVALENT MEASURES

1 medium lemon = 3 teaspoons grated
    peel
5 medium lemons = 1 cup juice
16 tablespoons = 1 cup
1 cup = 1/2 pint
4 cups = 1 quart
2 cups = 1 pound, "the world around"

LEMON TREES

A two year old was visiting her grandmother. "May I pick some eggs from your tree?"

The twist is that lemons contain life saving nutrients and eggs are life giving. They look like them, too!

Lemon trees are always green and have flowers and fruit almost continuously.

VARIETIES OF DWARF LEMON TREES
(4'-10' tall)

Man-Made Dwarfs

Type	Characteristics
Eureka	nearly thornless, almost seedless, tolerant to cold
Lisbon	Most vigorous
Ponderosa	Needs less light to produce

Natural Dwarf Lemons

Type	Characteristics
Meyer	flowers and fruit almost all year fruit less sour makes a good hedge

PICKING OR BUYING LEMONS

Look for smooth skins, free of blemishes and soft spots. The fruit should feel firm and heavy.

Pick lemons when green and 2-1/2" in diameter for best flavor and keeping quality.

Fruits and Vegetables

A For ASPARAGUS

1 pound asparagus
1/2 cup water
4 tablespoons fresh lemon juice

Cut ends of asparagus stalks on diagonal into 1/4" slices. Leave tips to small stalks whole. Cook in a coffee percolator so the stalks can stand upright. Add slices and then the small stalks to the water and lemon juice in the percolator. Cover to steam. Lower heat. Cook 5 to 10 minutes or until barely tender. Serve with sprinkling of lemon juice.

Makes 4 servings.

The Good News-Asparagus has only 65 calories per serving.

EASY SQUEEZE
For a convenient quick squeeze of lemon juice, warm the lemon for 20 seconds in the microwave before using a juicer or a faucet.

SUSIE'S TEWKESBURY SAUCE

1-1/2 tablespoons margarine
1-1/2 tablespoons lemon juice
1 teaspoon horseradish
1/4 teaspoon Dijon-style mustard
1/2 cup evaporated milk
Dash of white pepper.

Melt margarine in saucepan over low heat. Add lemon juice, horseradish, and mustard. Stir to combine. Add milk. Increase heat to medium. Cook. Whisk constantly until mixture thickens (4 to 5 minutes). Add pepper to taste. Serve immediately or keep hot in a thermos.

Makes 3/4 cup.

Tewkesbury is an old town near Worcester, where some of England's best fruits and vegetables are grown. This sauce is perfect over asparagus and other vegetables.

Serve sauce in a LEMON CUP
For a deeper cup cut only 1/4" from the top.

BOILED ARTICHOKES

4 artichokes
1 lemon for juice
1 lemon cut in thin slices
Bearnaise Sauce or mayonnaise

Wash artichokes. Cut off stems at base. Remove small bottom leaves and any discolored leaves. With knife, cut off one inch from top. With scissors, trim the points off the rest of the leaves. Rub all the cut edges with lemon to prevent discoloring. Remove chokes spreading the top leaves apart. Pull out the inner core of thistle like yellow leaves. Use a spoon to scrape out the hairy choke inside. Squeeze in a little lemon juice and press the artichoke back in shape. Place artichokes in a large saucepan. Add 2 inches water. Cover pan. Bring to boil on high heat. Reduce heat to low and cook 30 minutes. Artichokes are done when the bases can be easily pierced with a fork. Remove from saucepan with tongs. Drain upside down in a colander. Place on individual serving plates. Top each artichoke with a thin slice of lemon. Serve with Bearnaise Sauce or mayonnaise on the side.

Makes 4 servings.

Artichokes cook much faster in a microwave oven. Place in a round glass dish with a little water and cover loosely with plastic wrap. Cook on high until bases can be easily pierced with a fork.

BERNAISE SAUCE

3/4 cup margarine
2 egg yolks
2 tablespoons lemon juice
1 teaspoon tarragon vinegar
1 small clove of garlic
2 sprigs parsley

Stir egg yolks, lemon juice, and margarine over low heat. Be sure margarine melts slowly as this gives eggs time to cook and thicken the sauce without curdling. Add vinegar, minced garlic and minced parsley. Keep warm in a thermos until serving. Serve with artichokes or over steak.

Makes 1 cup.

Lemon juice can be substituted for wine or vinegar in any recipe.

baskets

Serve sauce in baskets. Cut a small slice off the bottom of the lemon so it will sit level. Cut away wedge shapes as shown. Carefully cut away fruit from "handle" leaving it attached to basket. Then cut out fruit from center. Scrape clean with large spoon. These can be made ahead and frozen in plastic bags until ready to use.

STEAMED GREEN BEANS

1 tablespoon oil
1 pound green beans, trimmed
1/2 cup diced sweet red pepper
2 tablespoons water
1/2 teaspoon basil leaves
1/8 teaspoon pepper
1 tablespoon lemon juice

In heavy skillet with a tight fitting lid place all ingredients except lemon juice. Cover and cook over medium heat, shaking pan occasionally to prevent sticking (15 to 18 minutes) or until tender-crisp. Toss with lemon juice.

Makes 4 servings.

Color and Lemon

Beans are tossed with lemon juice after steaming. Adding it before cooking to green vegetables dulls the color green.

BROCCOLI WITH LEMON CREAM

2 (10 ounce) pkgs. frozen broccoli
2 eggs
1/2 cup evaporated milk
3/4 cup mayonnaise
3 tablespoons lemon juice

Place broccoli in a buttered baking dish in one layer. Beat eggs with milk and mayonnaise until well blended. Add lemon juice. Pour mixture over the broccoli. Bake in a 350 degree oven for about 30 minutes. Sprinkle top of casserole with buttered bread crumbs. Bake for another 10 minutes or until browned. Garnish with a lemon twist.

Makes 8 servings.

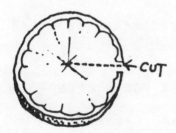
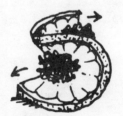

Sprinkle twist with paprika or-

parsley
broccoli flowerets
paprika
cherries
mint leaves

Paprika or parsley

HARVARD BEETS

3 cups diced or sliced cooked beets
1 teaspoon grated lemon peel
1/4 cup lemon juice
1/4 cup frozen orange
    juice concentrate
1 tablespoon cornstarch
1 tablespoon margarine

Drain beets. Heat 1/2 cup beet juice and frozen orange juice. Mix lemon juice and cornstarch. Stir into heated juices. Bring to a boil. Boil 1 minute. Add margarine, lemon peel and beets. Continue to heat until hot.

Makes 4 servings.

Lemon Enhances Some Colors

Red fruits and vegetables are enhanced in color by lemon juice.

HOLIDAY DINNER FOR A CROWD

*Pink or Green Lemonade
*Festive Salmon Ball
*Turkey Marco Polo
*Harvard Beets
*Lemon Rice
*Classic Waldorf Salad
*Pizza Fruit Pie
*Coffee Diable or *Perfect Cuppa Tea

lemon peel holly garnish

Dec 9-68

LEMON BUTTERED PEAS

2 pkgs. (10 ounces) frozen petite peas
1/4 cup margarine
3 lettuce leaves
2 lemons

Combine peas and margarine in a microwave dish. Dip lettuce leaves in water. Place over peas. Cover completely. Cover dish and microwave until tender, about 5 minutes. Discard lettuce leaves before serving. Cut lemons into quarters. Squeeze over each serving.

Makes 8 servings.

SPARKLING CARROTS

1 small onion, chopped
2 tablespoons margarine
1-1/2 pounds carrots,
    sliced 1/8" thick
1 cup lemon-lime carbonated beverage
1 tablespoon sugar

Saute onion in margarine in large saucepan. Add carrots and carbonated beverage. Season to taste with pepper. Add sugar and cook until liquid is absorbed and carrots are slightly glazed. Serve with a lemon wedge.

Makes 6 servings.

unpeeled wedges

BROILED TOMATOES

3 large tomatoes
2 tablespoons lemon juice
1/2 teaspoon garlic powder
1/4 cup grated parmesan cheese
1/4 cup minced fresh parsley

Wash tomatoes. Cut them crosswise into halves. Slice a small piece off the tops and bottoms. Dip them in lemon juice. Sprinkle with garlic powder and parmesan cheese. Broil for about 3 minutes or until tender. **Be careful not to burn tomato tops.** Sprinkle with parsley.

Makes 6 servings.

FAST FOOD MEAL

*Tuna Melt
*Broiled Tomatoes
Mixed green salad with
*Lively Lemon French Dressing
*Lemon Sherbet in a *Lemon Basket

LEMON BASKETS

SWEET POTATO DELIGHT

4 apples, peeled and sliced
1 (40-ounce) can of yams
4 bananas
2 lemons, grated peel and juice
1/2 teapoon cinnamon
6 tablespoons brown sugar
1/2 cup chopped pecans
    or sliced almonds
3 tablespoons margarine

Use canned yams or microwave fresh sweet potatoes until tender to a fork (about 5 minutes). Remove skin. Mash sweet potatoes with ripe bananas. Add grated lemon peel and 4 tablespoons lemon juice. Top with apple slices that have been tossed in juice of lemon. Sprinkle with cinnamon, sugar and nuts. Dot with margarine. Bake covered, at 350 degrees for 30 minutes. Uncover. Bake 15 minutes longer. Serve piping hot.

Makes 8 servings.

GRATING ALTERNATIVE
An alternative to grating is to use the blender or food processor.
Wash the fruit. Score and peel it. Cut peel in slivers. Cut the fruit in half and seed it. Process the lemon and peel. Use the whole fruit!

LEMON RICE

1 cup uncooked rice
1-1/2 cups boiling water
1/2 lemon, peel and juice
1/4 cup margarine
3/4 cup evaporated milk, warmed
chopped parsley

Add rice to boiling water. Cook. Cover over medium heat until rice is tender. Stir occasionally, about 20 minutes. Do not over cook. Saute lemon peel in margarine about 3 minutes. Remove peel. Add margarine to cooked rice. Add lemon juice gradually. Toss until seasoned to taste. Add half of warmed milk. Fold gently. Add enough additional milk to coat all grains of rice. Place in oven proof serving dish and keep warm until serving time. Garnish with chopped parsley and a lemon curl.

Makes 6 servings.

When cooking white vegetables lemon juice makes them whiter.

curls

Cut half of fruit from cartwheel. Leave entire peel. Curl peel to center.

SWEET AND SOUR RED CABBAGE

1 head red cabbage
1 sliced red onion
1/4 cup lemon juice
1/4 cup water
1 tablespoon sugar or sugar substitute

Shred red cabbage. Cook, with 1 sliced red onion, in lemon juice and water. When tender crunchy, remove from the heat. Add sugar substitute.

Makes 8 servings.

SCANDINAVIAN DINNER

*Swedish Fruit Soup
*Speedy Swedish Meatballs
Noodles
*Lemon Poppy Seed Muffins
*Sweet and Sour Red Cabbage
*Lemon Buttered Peas
Danish Applecake

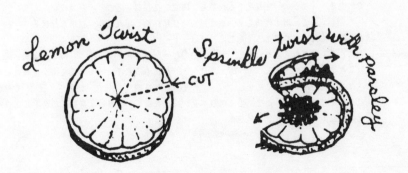

Lemon Twist — CUT — Sprinkle twist with parsley

CRISP CUCUMBER SLICES IN MOCK CHAMPAGNE

    1 cucumber
    1/2 cup vinegar
    1/2 cup lemon-lime carbonated beverage
    2 teaspoons lemon juice

Remove part of the cucumber skin with a vegetable peeler. Score the sides with the tines of a fork. Cut cucumber in thin slices. Cover the slices with ice cubes. Let stand 1/2 hour. Drain and remove ice. Add vinegar, lemon-lime carbonated beverage and lemon juice to the cucumber slices. Put bowl in refrigerator and marinate a couple of hours. Drain before serving.

Makes 4 servings.

"Pass The Lemon! Reducing Sodium Without Reducing The Flavor

Most Americans consume two to three times the amount of sodium recommended as 'safe and adequate'.

There are ways for you to reduce your sodium intake and still enjoy your food:

1. Stop adding salt to your food. About one fourth of our sodium intake comes from the salt we add to food.

2. Eliminate or reduce the amount of salt in your recipes."

Elizabeth Shiply-Moses, M.S.R.D. nutritionist with Kaiser Permanente Health Care Program in the Washington/Baltimore Area. Roslyn/Balston Review, May, 1988

no salt is added to any recipe in *Lemon Twist.*

VEGGIES

Asparagus
Tiny Brussels Sprouts
Button Mushrooms
Broccoli flowers
Carrot curls or sticks
Cucumber wheels or sticks
Radish roses
Cherry Tomatoes
Jicama sticks
Baby corn
Celery fans
Zucchini slices
Cauliflowerets
Avocado chunks dipped in lemon bath

Clean and prepare vegetables. Cut into convenient sizes for finger foods. Chill until crisp. Serve in a lettuce lined basket with a large lemon shell in the middle with dip*.

Makes 1 serving per 1/2 cup.

Ascorbic acid in lemon juice has the magic to prevent oxygen in the air from reaching fruits and vegetables and turning them brown.
*A **lemon bath** of 1/4 cup lemon juice and 1 cup water will prevent browning.*

Health and Nutrition
"Lemon juice is used in medicine for anti hemorraging, plasma extender, and intestinal disorders."
Encyclopedia Brittanica, 1975

GLAZED CARROTS AND ONIONS

8 medium carrots
1 cup water
12 small whole white onions
3 tablespoons margarine
3 tablespoons apricot preserves
1/4 cup lemon juice
2 tablespoons chopped parsley

Scrape and wash carrots. Cut diagonally into 1/2 inch thick slices. Peel onions and cut a small cross in root end of each to help keep onions whole during cooking. Bring water to a boil. Add carrots and onions. Reduce heat. Cook covered for 10 minutes until tender. Drain. Melt margarine and apricot preserves with lemon juice. Add to vegetables and stir gently over low heat until evenly glazed and heated through. Sprinkle with parsley. Serve with lemon sauce.

Makes 12 servings.

SAVORY LEMON SAUCE

1 cup mayonnaise
2 tablespoons lemon juice

Combine mayonnaise and juice. Mix well. Serve in a large lemon cup on the side.

Makes 1 cup.

Note: *This tangy sauce is equally delicious on asparagus, broccoli, mushrooms, green beans, peas or carrots. A great sauce on broiled fish, too!*

VEGETABLE KABOBS

2 carrots, cut in 1 inch lengths
4 medium zucchini, 1 inch cuts
4 medium yellow squash, cut
16 fresh mushrooms, whole
16 cherry tomatoes, whole
2 green peppers, cut in 2" squares
1/4 cup margarine
1 tablespoon Worcestershire sauce
2 tablespoons lemon juice
1/4 teaspoon lemon pepper

Cook carrots in small amount of boiling water 10 minutes or until tender-crisp. Alternate on 8 skewers with carrots, zucchini, yellow squash, mushrooms, tomatoes, and green peppers. Melt margarine. Add Worcestershire sauce, lemon juice and lemon pepper. Brush kabobs with lemon mixture. Grill or broil 5 minutes. Turn occasionally. Or bake in 400 degree oven 10 minutes.

Makes 8 servings.

PLEASE PASS THE LEMON

For those who prefer more seasoning serve a lemon that is plugged with a juicer. Or roll lemon on counter. Poke hole in one end with a tooth pick. Pass the lemon to squeeze out what you need. Replace toothpick. Refrigerate until you need another squeeze.

Only 3 calories a squeeze!

A GRAND TRADITION

Possibly the most sought-after Christmas dinner in America features boar's head and peacock pie. It's hosted by an English nobleman named Squire Bracebridge, a fictional character, the creation of writer Washington Irving nearly 170 years ago. For the last 60 years it has been re-enacted at the Ahwahnee Hotel in Yosemite National Park.

Our family enjoys putting on our version at home. The menu is below. The recipes are in this book you are holding.

BRACEBRIDGE CELEBRATION FEAST

*Caviar Pie and beverage of choice
(Announce with trumpet sound
DINNER TO BE SERVED)

(Announce **Soup** with a bowl of lemons)
*Lemon Tree Soup

(Announce **Fish Course** with a "fish")
*Shrimp Scampi and *Broiled Tomatoes

(Announce ***Peacock Pie** waving feathers)
*Magic Ink Trick

(Announce **Boar's Head (Ham)** with a bear)
*Ham with Pineapple Sauce
*Steamed Green Beans

(Announce **Salad** with a bowl of greens)
Grapefruit and Avocado Salad
*Lemon Honey Dressing

(Announce with **candle and singing**)
*Lemon Cake Roll and *Cafe Napoli

(Announce **toasts** to follow)
*Crock Pot Wassail

HERB LEMON SAUCE
FOR ZUCCHINI
(or any other favorite vegetable)

1 tablespoon corn starch
1 cup milk
2 tablespoons margarine
1/8 teaspoon pepper
2-1/2 tablespoons lemon juice
3 tablespoons snipped fresh dill or
    1 teaspoon dry dill
1 drop yellow food color
1 tablespoon chopped parsley.

In saucepan mix corn starch and milk until smooth. Add margarine, pepper and lemon juice. Stir. Bring to boil over medium heat. Boil 1 minute. Remove from heat. Add dill, yellow food color and parsley. Pour over cooked zucchini, asparagus, broccoli, or any other favorite vegetable.

Makes 1-1/3 cups.

Give a jar of this sauce with label and this book along with zucchini or any other vegetable you grow abundantly in your garden. A special touch for a friend!

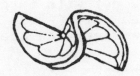

GRILLED BANANAS

1 banana
1/4 teaspoon cinnamon
2 teaspoons sugar
2 teaspoons lemon juice

Peel banana. Place on square of buttered heavy foil. Sprinkle with lemon juice, cinnamon, and sugar. Wrap tightly. Grill 6 inches from coals about 10 minutes.

Makes 1 serving per banana.

BAKED BANANAS

4 bananas
4 tablespoons margarine
4 tablespoons brown sugar
2 teaspoons lemon juice

Peel bananas and cut them in half the long way. Arrange in a shallow greased baking dish. Sprinkle with brown sugar, lemon juice and dot with margarine. Bake in a 350 degree oven for 10 minutes. Delicious served over ice cream!

Makes 4 servings.

APPLESAUCE WHIP

1 envelope unflavored gelatin
   (pre-measured to gel 2 cups
   of liquid)
1/2 cup cold water
2 packets Equal or 4 teaspoons sugar
3 ice cubes
2 tablespoons lemon juice
2 cups cold, unsweetened applesauce

Sprinkle gelatin on cold water in saucepan to soften. Place over medium heat. Stir constantly until gelatin is dissolved, about 2 minutes. Remove from heat. Blend in sugar and ice cubes, until cubes melt. Add lemon juice and applesauce. Beat with rotary beater until light. Turn into serving dishes. Sprinkle with cinnamon.

Makes 6 servings.

APPLESAUCE

6-8 apples, peeled, cored and cut
2 teaspoons lemon juice
1/4 cup water
1/2 cup sugar

Add lemon juice, water and sugar to apples in microwave dish. Cover. Microwave until apples are soft. Process in a blender for a smooth applesauce or break up with a fork for a chunky applesauce. Serve with a dash of cinnamon on top.

Makes 4 cups.

FAKE PINEAPPLE

4 quarts grated or diced zucchini
1-1/2 cups "Real Lemon" juice
1 can (46 ounces)
    unsweetened pineapple juice
3 cups sugar

Remove peeling and seeds from zucchini. Grate or dice. Mix all ingredients thoroughly. Simmer for 20 minutes. Stir frequently. Pour hot zucchini mixture into clean, hot jars, leaving 1/2-inch head space. Process 30 minutes in boiling water bath.

"Ball Test Kitchens and Purdue University extension specialist, Jean Howe, developed this "Zucchini-Pineapple" to assure safety of a very popular recipe."
Food Preservation News'Notes, Spring 1982, Ball Corp.

Where Are The Lemons?
"Southern California harvests about 95% of the USA's lemons.
The United States produces 43% of the world's supply of lemons. Italy produces 45% of the lemons. The rest of the world produces the other 12%."
Encyclopedia Brittanica, 1986

Desserts

LEMON FILLING

2 cups sugar
1/2 cup cornstarch
1-1/2 cups water
4 egg yolks
2 tablespoons margarine
2/3 cup lemon juice
3 tablespoons grated lemon peel

Combine 1 cup sugar and cornstarch in top of double boiler. Gradually blend in water. Cook over boiling water, stirring constantly, until thickened. Cover and cook 10 minutes longer, stirring occasionally. Meanwhile beat egg yolks and remaining 1 cup sugar. Blend a little hot mixture into egg yolks, then stir into remaining hot mixture. Cook 2 minutes more. Remove from heat. Add margarine, lemon juice and peel. Cool before filling cake.

COCONUT CREAM FROSTING

1 teaspoon unflavored gelatin
2 tablespoons cold water
1 pint whipping cream
3 tablespoons powdered sugar
1/2 teaspoon vanilla
2 cups flake coconut

Soften gelatin in 2 tablespoons cold water. Dissolve in 2 tablespoons hot cream. Chill until slightly thickened. Beat until smooth. Using high speed, whip remaining whipping cream until small peaks form. Then turn down and continue beating until just stiff. Add whipped gelatin mixture, powdered sugar and vanilla. Frost cake. Sprinkle with coconut. Decorate with strawberries and lemon twists.

LEMON LAYER COCONUT CAKE

2 (18.5 ounce) packages White Cake Mix
1-1/3 cups water
2/3 cup lemon juice
4 egg whites
Lemon Filling
Coconut Cream Frosting

Using the above ingredients follow directions on packages for mixing.

Divide dough between three 8" layer cake pans. Bake according to directions on package. Cool.

Spread Lemon Filling (p.158) between layers of cake. Frost sides and top of cake with Coconut Cream Frosting (p.158). Garnish with strawberries and/or lemon twists.

Makes 20 servings.

This is the ultimate classy cake!

Lemon Twists

Lemon juice added to any cake makes it taste fresher. Just decrease the amount of other liquid by amount of lemon juice.

LEMON CAKE ROLL

1/2 cup flour
1/2 teaspoon baking powder
4 eggs, separated
1/2 cup + 1/3 cup sugar
1 tablespoon lemon juice
1/3 cup powdered sugar

Preheat oven to 350 degrees. Grease and flour a 15-1/2 x 10-1/2 x 1 inch jelly roll pan. Line bottom with wax paper. Beat egg whites and lemon juice until frothy. Gradually add 1/2 cup sugar until glossy. Set aside. Sift flour and baking powder together. Beat eggs yolks until thickened and beat in 1/3 cup sugar. Fold into egg whites. Fold into dry ingredients just until blended. Spread batter in pan. Bake 12 to 15 minutes until lightly browned. Loosen edges and immediately turn upside down on a cotton towel generously sprinkled with powdered sugar. Remove paper. Trim off stiff edges. While hot, roll cake and towel from narrow end. Cool. Unroll cake. Spread with cool lemon filling to within 1/2 " from edge. Reroll (without towel). Trim off ends.

Makes 8 servings.

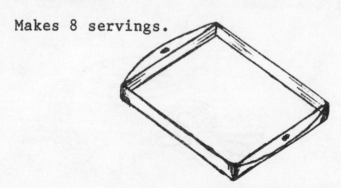

jelly roll pan

LEMONY O.J. FILLING

2/3 cup sugar
1-1/2 tablespoons cornstarch
1/2 cup orange juice
1/4 cup lemon juice
3 egg yolks
1 tablespoon margarine
1/2 teaspoon grated lemon peel

Combine sugar and cornstarch. Mix well. Stir in egg yolks, orange and lemon juices. Cook and stir over medium heat until mixture comes to a boil. Reduce heat. Cook 1/2 minute longer. Remove from heat. Stir in margarine and lemon peel. Let cool at room temperature until set (about 1-1/2 hours). Open cake roll. Spread with lemony filling. Reroll.

Sift powdered sugar on top of cake roll. Decorate with lemon twists and mint leaves.

The Real Gold

"Commercial citrus orchards were not planted in Southern California until advice came from the North to the South to plant citrus after the Gold Rush in the mid 1800's. The reason: more people suffered and died from scurvy than from the terrible epidemic of cholera (10,000) during the Gold Rush." The twist is that the "real gold" in California is in lemons!
Kenneth Carpenter, *The History of Scurvy and Vitamin C*

ALL-AMERICAN LEMON CAKE

1 (3 ounce) package lemon gelatin mix
3/4 cup water
1 (18.5 ounce) yellow cake mix
    or pudding-included cake mix)
1/2 cup oil
4 eggs
1 teaspoon lemon juice
Pour Topping

Mix gelatin, water, cake mix, oil, eggs, and lemon juice. Pour batter into 13 X 9 baking pan that is greased and floured. Bake at 350 degrees for 40 to 45 minutes.
Punch holes in cake with toothpick or fork. Pour on Topping.

POUR TOPPING

1 cup powdered sugar
1/3 cup lemon juice

Blend powdered sugar with lemon juice. Pour on hot cake after pricking.

Makes 12 servings.

This is a time-honored American Lemon Cake Recipe developed by General Foods Corp. in 1958. It has been updated with new cake mixes.

CARROT CAKE WITH LEMON CREAM FROSTING

3 cups flour
2 cups sugar
2 teaspoons cinnamon
1-1/2 teaspoons soda
1 teaspoon baking powder
3 eggs
1-1/2 cups salad oil
1 can (8 ounces) crushed
    pineapple, drained
2 cups grated carrots
1-1/2 cups chopped walnuts or pecans
1 teaspoon lemon juice

Combine flour, sugar, cinnamon, soda, and baking powder. Drain pineapple, saving syrup. Mix syrup, eggs, and oil. Add dry ingredients. Stir in pineapple, carrots, nuts and lemon juice. Turn into greased 13 x 9 inch pan. Bake for 50 minutes or until it springs back at a light touch. Cool before frosting, cutting and serving.

Makes 12 servings.

LEMON CREAM FROSTING

1 (3 ounce) package cream cheese
1/2 cup or 1 stick of margarine
2 tablespoons lemon juice
1-1/2 teaspoons grated lemon peel
1 (1 pound) box powdered sugar

Beat cream cheese and margarine until fluffy. Blend in lemon juice, peel and sugar. Beat until smooth and creamy.

Makes frosting for one 13 x 9 inch cake.

SHIRLEY'S GOLDEN ANGEL CAKE

1 package angel food cake mix
1-1/2 cups water
2 tablespoons lemon juice
1 tablespoon grated lemon peel
6 drops yellow food coloring

Blend cake ingredients in large bowl. **Do not overbeat.** Pour into ungreased tube pan. Bake at 325 degrees on lowest oven rack for 45 minutes or until crust is a deep golden brown and cracks are dry. Invert cake and cool in pan at least 1 hour. Remove from pan carefully.

GLAZE

2 cups powdered sugar
1 tablespoon milk
2 tablespoons lemon juice
1 tablespoon margarine
1 tablespoon grated lemon peel

In a small bowl blend all glaze ingredients until smooth. If too thick, stir in additional lemon juice, a drop at a time. Spoon over cake allowing to drizzle down sides. Decorate with lemon cartwheel twists.

Makes 12 servings.

cartwheel twists

Cut unpeeled cartwheel just to center and twist.

LEMON MERINGUE PIE

1-1/2 cups sugar
1/4 cup plus 2 teaspoons cornstarch
3/4 cup lemon juice
1/4 cup cold water
5 egg yolks, well beaten
2 tablespoons margarine
1-1/4 cups boiling water
3 teaspoons grated lemon peel
4 drops yellow food color
Mile High Meringue
1 baked 9-inch Z-Best Pie Crust

Mix sugar and cornstarch using a wire whisk. Blend in lemon juice and cold water. Add egg yolks and margarine. Gradually add boiling water, stirring with rubber spatula. Bring to full boil, stirring constantly over medium heat. Reduce heat slightly as mixture begins to thicken. Boil for 1 minute. Stir in grated peel and food coloring. Pour into baked pie crust.

MILE HIGH MERINGUE

5 egg whites, at room temperature
  to make larger volume
1/2 teaspoon cream of tartar
1/2 cup sugar

Beat egg whites until frothy. Add cream of tartar. Beat on high speed until whites will bend over slightly when beaters are withdrawn. Gradually add sugar and beat until whites are stiff. Place meringue on pie filling. Push gently against inner edge of pie crust, sealing edges well. Bake in 350 degree oven for 15 minutes or until golden brown. Cool at least 2 hours before cutting.

Makes 1 pie.

HEAVENLY LEMON PIE

MERINGUE SHELL

4 egg whites
1/8 teaspoon cream of tartar
1 cup sugar

Beat egg whites until foamy. Add cream of tartar and sugar, a little at a time. Beating until the meringue is stiff and glossy. Pour meringue into a heavily greased 9 inch pie pan. Smooth it with a spatula. Bake in a 275 degree oven for 1 hour. Cool.

LEMON FILLING

4 egg yolks
1/2 cup sugar
1/4 cup lemon juice, freshly squeezed
1 tablespoon finely grated lemon peel
1 pint whipping cream, whipped
2 tablespoons powdered sugar

Beat egg yolks. On the top of a double boiler, cook the egg yolks with the sugar, lemon juice and lemon peel. Cook and stir until mixture thickens. Cool. Fold in half of whipped cream. Turn into meringue crust. Refrigerate at last 2 hours to set. Fold powdered sugar into remaining whipped cream. Spread over chilled pie. Sprinkle grated lemon peel on top of pie just before serving.

Makes 6 servings.

Substitute for Cream of Tartar
1/2 teaspoon lemon juice = 1/8 teaspoon cream of tartar.

LEMON CURD

4 large lemons
2 cups sugar
1 cup margarine
8 eggs, slightly beaten

With peeler, pare peel from lemons. Set aside. Squeeze lemons for 1 cup juice. Combine peel and juice with sugar, margarine and eggs in top of double boiler. Cook over simmering water for 20 to 30 minutes. Stir occasionally until a thick pudding like consistency. Strain. Keep refrigerated up to 1 month.

Makes 4 cups.

Specialty gourmet shops carry lemon curd. Lemon curd is a thick, eggy, tart-sweet mixture. It can be used as a filling for cakes, cookie sandwiches, tartlets, sweet rolls or as a spread for hot breads. It's also known as lemon cheese.

TOM THUMB LEMON TARTS
Make or buy tart shells. To make tart shells buy All Ready Pie Crusts in the refrigerator section of the market. Cut pastry in circles. Fit into small tart or muffin pans. Press edges thoroughly with fork to prevent puffing. Bake at 450 degrees from 6 to 8 minutes. Cool. Fill with lemon curd. Garnish with a slice of kumquat and lime. Refrigerate until served.

lemon border

"Z" BEST PIE CRUST

2 cups flour
3/4 cup cold shortening
1 egg
6 tablespoons cold lemon juice

Blend flour and shortening with 2 knives or pastry blender until dough is size of small peas. Break egg into measuring cup. Beat. Add lemon juice. Blend to flour-shortening mixture with fork. Seal dough in plastic wrap. Refrigerate. Use as needed. (Pastry dough keeps up to 2 months.)

Makes 1 (2-crust) or 2 (1-crust) pies.
ONE CRUST PIE
1-1/4 cups cold pie crust mix

Make a ball with pie crust mix. Put dough between plastic sheets. Flatten ball as much as possible with your hands. Roll as thin as possible with rolling pin into a circle 1" bigger than pie pan. Ease crust into pan. Gently press toward center to avoid stretching. Press firmly against sides and bottom.
Fold under edge of crust along pan edge. Flute edge with fork to prevent shrinking. Trim crust even with edge of pan.
UNFILLED CRUST: Generously prick the bottom and sides with fork.
Bake at 450 degrees for 9 to 11 minutes or until lightly browned. Cool before filling.
FILLED CRUST: Do not prick. Fill and bake according to your favorite recipe.
TWO CRUST PIE: Follow directions for crust with "Z" Best Apple Pie.

"Z"-BEST APPLE PIE

2 cups apples, peeled, cored and
   thinly sliced
2 tablespoons water
2 tablespoons lemon juice
1/2 cup sugar
1/2 cup brown sugar
2 tablespoons flour
1/2 teaspoon cinnamon
1/16 teaspoon nutmeg
2 (9-inch) pie crusts

Sprinkle apples with water and lemon juice. Microwave 2 minutes. Mix apples with brown sugar, flour, cinnamon, and nutmeg. Turn apple filling into pastry. Trim overhanging edge of pastry 1/2 inch from rim of pan. Roll second round of dough. Fold into quarters. Cut slits so steam can escape. Place over filling and unfold. Trim overhanging edge of pastry 1 inch from rim of pan. Fold and roll top edge under lower edge. Press on rim to seal with tines of fork. Brush top crust with evaporated milk for a glaze. Cover edge with 3 inch strip of aluminum foil to prevent excess browning. Remove foil last 15 minutes of baking. Bake in 450 degree oven for 10 minutes. Then bake at 350 degrees for 40 minutes.

Makes 8 servings.

FRUIT PIZZA PIE

1 roll refrigerator sugar cookies
1/2 cup sugar
2 tablespoons corn starch
1-1/2 cups apple juice
1 teaspoon grated lemon peel
1/4 cup lemon juice
6 cups assorted sliced fresh fruit:
    such as: kiwis, apples with peel,
    strawberries, grapes, bananas,
    orange sections, pears, melon
8 ounces cream cheese, softened
4 tablespoons milk
1/4 cup sugar

Cut room temperature cookie dough in half. Place half of the dough on each of two cookie sheets or pizza pans. Flatten with your hands. Put wax paper on top of dough and roll into a smooth circle. Put a 10" plate on top and mark for a circle. Trim away excess. Bake 10-12 minutes at 350 degrees. Cool. Mix sugar and corn starch. Gradually stir in apple juice until smooth. Stir constantly. Bring to boil over medium heat. Boil one minute. Remove from heat. Stir in lemon peel and lemon juice. Cool. Fold in fruit that turns brown (apples, bananas, and pears. Spread cream cheese and sugar thinned with milk on each of the cookie crust pastries. Arrange fruit on top. Drizzle glaze on fruit. Chill 4 hours or until set.

Makes 14 servings.

SHAKER LEMON PIE

2 large lemons
2 cups sugar
4 eggs, beaten
9-inch two crust pastry

Slice lemons paper thin, including peel. Combine with sugar. Mix well. Let stand at least 2 hours or preferably overnight. Mix occasionally. Fold in beaten eggs. Mix well. Arrange slices evenly in 9-inch pie shell. Cover with top crust. Cut several slits near center. Bake at 450 degrees for 15 minutes. Reduce heat. Bake at 375 degrees for 20 minutes longer or until knife inserted near center comes out clean. Cool.

Makes 8 servings.

CHOCOLATE LEAVES

12 lemon leaves
1 cup semisweet chocolate bits

Wash lemon leaves. Dry with paper towels. Melt chocolate in microwave 1-1/2 minutes. Stir. With knife spread chocolate on **underside** of each leaf. (The underside provides the best vein markings.) Avoid getting chocolate on the front of the leaf: it will make removal difficult. Chill until firm.

Carefully peel leaves away from chocolate. Cover and refrigerate until ready to use.

IMPOSSIBLE LEMON PIE

1 cup milk
1 cup sugar
3/4 cup lemon juice
1 tablespoon grated lemon peel
1/2 cup buttermilk biscuit mix
4 eggs
1/4 cup margarine, diced

Put milk, sugar, lemon juice, lemon peel, biscuit mix, eggs and margarine in blender or food processor. Blend 2 to 3 minutes. Pour batter into buttered 10 inch pie pan. Bake at 350 degrees for 40 minutes, or until center of pie is set. Sprinkle 1/2 teaspoon sugar over top of baked pie. Place under broiler until lightly browned. Cool and serve with Whipped Topping, #2.

Makes 8 servings.

WHIPPED TOPPING, #2

2/3 cup evaporated milk
1/4 cup sugar
2 teaspoons lemon juice

Pour milk into small mixer bowl. Place in freezer until ice crystals form around edge, about 30 minutes. Add sugar and lemon juice. Beat until very thick and fluffy. Serve immediately. Topping can be refrigerated 1 hour or frozen for future use.
Makes 1-1/2 cups.

....Only 10 calories per tablespoon and a good source of calcium!

LEMON-ORANGE CREAM

1 (4-1/2 ounce) package lemon pudding
   and pie filling
2 cups water
2 egg yolks
1/4 cup sugar
1 tablespoon lemon juice
1/2 pint orange yogurt or
   other flavor yogurt
1/2 cup whipping cream, whipped with
2 tablespoons powdered sugar
1 can Mandarin oranges
6 lemon twists

Combine pudding mix, egg yolks, and 1/4 cup water in sauce pan. Blend well. Add remaining water, sugar and lemon juice. Cook and stir until mixture comes to a full boil and is thickened, about 5 minutes. Remove from heat. Cool. Just before serving, beat until smooth. Fold in yogurt. Spoon into sherbet glasses or pie shell. Serve topped with sweetened whipped cream, Mandarin oranges and a lemon twist.

Makes 6 servings.

A really smooth dessert or pie filling.

WENDY'S PETITE CHEESE CAKES

2 (8 ounces) packages cream cheese
3/4 cup sugar
1 egg
1 tablespoon lemon juice
24 vanilla wafers
1 can cherry pie filling

Preheat oven to 375 degrees. Beat eggs, sugar, cream cheese, and lemon juice until fluffy. Fill a muffin tin with paper cups. Place vanilla wafer in bottom of each. Fill cups 2/3 full with cheese mixture. Bake 15-20 minutes. Top each with three cherries and pie filling.

Makes 24 servings.

These are easily carried to a party or picnic in muffin pans.

AMERICAN BANNER DESSERT

Top half of the cheese cakes with blueberry pie filling and half with cherry pie filling. Put Whipped Topping on 1/3 of all cakes. Place on a doily lined tray in a diagonal design with red, white and blue cheese cakes.

Makes 24 servings.

ANGEL WHISPERS

1/2 cup margarine
2 eggs
1 tablespoon lemon juice
1/2 cup sugar
3/4 cup plus 2 tablespoons sifted
   flour
3/4 cup cornstarch
2 teaspoons baking powder
1/2 cup powdered sugar

Preheat oven to 400 degrees. Beat margarine, eggs, lemon juice and sugar together. Combine with flour, cornstarch, and baking powder. Drop by 1/2 teaspoon onto ungreased cookie sheet. Bake in oven at 400 degrees for 10 minutes. Put two cookies together sandwich style using Lemon Butter as the filling. Roll in powdered sugar.

Makes 5 dozen.

Substitute for Lemon Juice
(In a pinch)
1/4 teaspoon lemon extract and 1/2 cup water. Check flavor. Makes 1/2 cup.

LEMON BUTTER

1 egg
2/3 cup sugar
1-1/2 tablespoons margarine
3 tablespoons lemon juice

Beat ingredients together. Cook over low heat until thickened. Stir occasionally.

They look expensive!

BAKLAVA
SYRUP

Prepare syrup first so that it may be cooling.

1-1/2 cups sugar
1 cup water
5 whole cloves
1 cinnamon stick
1/2 cup honey
1 tablespoon lemon juice

Mix all ingredients. Bring to a boil for 5 minutes. Cool.

BASE

4 cups (1 pound) ground walnuts
1/2 cup sugar
1 teaspoon cinnamon
1/2 pound filo dough
1 cup butter, melted

Preheat oven to 325 degrees. In large bowl combine walnuts, sugar, cinnamon and allspice. Trim filo to 15-1/2 x 10-1/2 inches. To prevent drying, keep filo covered with plastic wrap as you work.

Brush a 15-1/2" x 10-1/2" jelly roll pan (a pan like a cookie sheet with narrow sides) with melted butter. Place one sheet of filo in pan. Brush with butter. Layer and butter 5 more sheets of filo. Sprinkle with 1-1/2 cups nut mixture. Layer and butter 2 more sheets. Sprinkle with 1 cup nut mixture. Repeat,topping nut layer with 6 sheets of buttered filo. Brush remaining butter over all. Trim edges. Cut into diamond shapes in pan. Bake in 325 degree oven for 1 hour. Check. Bake 10 to 15 minutes more if necessary until top is light brown. Pour cool syrup over hot baklava. Cool 5 hours.

Makes 40 bars.

TEMPLE CITY LEMON BARS

2 cups flour
1 cup margarine
1/2 cup powdered sugar
4 eggs, well beaten
2 cups sugar
6 tablespoons lemon juice
grated peel of 2 lemons
4 tablespoons flour
1 teaspoon baking powder

Preheat oven to 350 degrees. Mix 2 cups flour, margarine, and powdered sugar until crumbly like pie crust. Pat into a 13 X 9 inch glass baking dish. Bake 20 minutes. Beat eggs with sugar, lemon juice, peel, flour and baking soda. Pour over hot crust. Bake 20 minutes at 350 degrees. Cool. Sift powdered sugar over the top. Cut into bars.

Makes 36 bars.

Sequence to make it easier. . .

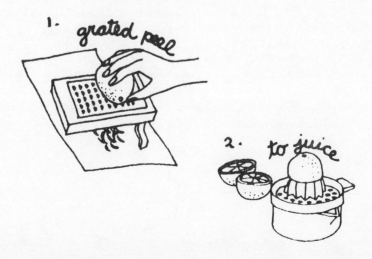

1. grated peel

2. to juice

LEMON FRUIT SLICES

1 cup margarine
1 cup sugar
2 eggs
2 teaspoons lemon juice
1-1/2 teaspoons grated lemon peel
3 cups flour
Food colors (yellow, green and orange)
Colored sugars (yellow, green
  and orange)

Mix margarine, sugar, eggs and lemon juice. Blend in flour. Divide dough into 1/4 part to remain plain. The large part, work in yellow food color and the lemon peel. If desired, separate the large part into 3 equal parts and work in 3 different colors. Cover dough. Chill 1 hour.

Shape each colored dough into roll, 2 inches in diameter and 4 inches long. For even baking make each roll the exact length and diameter by using a tape measure or ruler. Divide plain dough into 3 equal parts. Roll each part into a rectangle, 6x4 inches. Wrap one rectangle around each roll of colored dough. Press together firmly. Roll in matching colored sugar. Wrap. Chill at least 4 hours. Cut rolls into 1/8-inch slices. Place on ungreased baking sheet. Cut each slice in half. Bake at 400 degrees for 7 minutes. Remove immediately from baking sheet to wire rack.

Makes 10 dozen cookies.

LEMON APRICOT BARS

1 cup dried apricots, chopped
1/4 cup brown sugar
1 cup water
1 teaspoon lemon juice
1/2 cup flaked or shredded coconut

Combine apricots, sugar, water and lemon juice. Cook over low heat until thick. Stir frequently. Add coconut. Cool.

CRUMB BASE AND TOPPING

1/2 cup flour
1/2 teaspoon soda
1/2 cup brown sugar
1 cup oats (quick or old fashioned, uncooked)
1/3 cup margarine, melted
1 teaspoon grated lemon peel

Preheat oven to 350 degrees. Sift flour and soda into bowl. Stir in sugar and oats. Add margarine. Mix until mixture is crumbly.
Press half of crumb mixture into greased 8-inch square baking pan. Spread with filling. Cover with remaining crumb mixture. Press lightly. Bake in 350 degree oven for 25 minutes. Cool and cut into bars.

Makes 2 dozen.

A Long Term Investment
"A lemon tree bears fruit 4 years after grafting and some continue to bear for 50 years."
World Book Encyclopedia, 1986

LEMON CRISPS

1 (18 ounce) yellow or white cake mix
1/2 cup cooking oil
2 eggs
1 teaspoon grated lemon peel
1 tablespoon lemon juice

Combine all ingredients and mix well.
Drop from a teaspoon onto an ungreased
cookie sheet.
Bake at 350 degrees for 10 minutes or
until golden brown.
Cool on cookie sheet for about 1
minute, then remove to rack to finish
cooling.
Cool before frosting.

Makes 5 dozen, 2 inch cookies.

LEMON FROSTING

2 tablespoons margarine
2 cups powdered sugar
3 tablespoons lemon juice
1 lemon, grated peel
1 drop yellow food coloring.

Combine first three ingredients. Beat
until light and creamy.
Stir in grated lemon peel and food
coloring.
Frost when cookies are cool.

*When a recipe calls for dropping dough
by the teaspoonful, make sure to use a
tableware teaspoon, not a measuring
teaspoon. The latter will result in much
smaller cookies.*

*Most cookies will freeze well. Simply
place in freezerproof (air tight)
containers. Label and date. Cookies will
keep for up to three months.*

MEXICAN BANNER DESSERT

1 (6 ounces) package red gelatin
1 (3 ounces) package lemon gelatin
1 cup whipped topping*
1 (6 ounces) package lime gelatin

Prepare red gelatin according to package instructions. Turn into greased 9 x 13 inch glass dish. Chill until firm. Prepare lemon gelatin in separate bowl. Chill until partially jelled. Fold in whipped topping. Pour over red gelatin. Chill until firm. Prepare lime gelatin. Spoon over first two layers. Refrigerate until firm. Cut into squares to serve. Garnish with a lemon twist.

Makes 10 servings.

Colorful and light to serve after a Mexican meal.

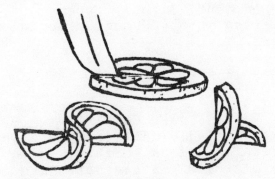

LEMON TWIST
Cut cartwheel to center and twist.

LEMON SOUFFLE

3 lemons
4 eggs
1/2 cup sugar
2 cups milk
1 teaspoon vanilla
2 tablespoons flour

This recipe is prepared in two stages, syrup and base.

To prepare the syrup, squeeze the juice from the lemons and scrape the peels clean of leftover fruit. Mince the peels as finely as possible. Put the peels, lemon juice and one tablespoon of sugar into saucepan. Cook this mixture until it becomes a syrup. Set it aside.

For the base, heat the milk and vanilla in a saucepan. Separate the whites and yolks of the eggs. Mix the rest of the sugar with the egg yolks. Add the flour to the yolks and sugar. When the milk begins to boil, add the yolk mixture to it. Continue to cook for about one minute, stirring often. When the mixture thickens, take it off the heat and add the syrup. Beat the egg whites stiff but not dry. Fold them into the base. Pour the whole thing into a buttered and lightly sugared souffle dish. Bake in a 400 degree oven for 15 minutes.

Makes 4 servings.

NEW CUISINE
Bake in individual souffle dishes with berries in season. Serve on a dinner plate with a miniature rose and a mint leaf.

MARY'S FROZEN LEMONADE WHIP

1-1/2 cups finely crushed vanilla
   wafer crumbs
6 tablespoons melted margarine
1 (6 ounces) can frozen lemonade
1 (6 ounces) can water
1/2 pound (32 marshmallows)-or
   10 miniature marshmallows equal 1
   regular size
1/2 pint heavy cream, whipped

Combine vanilla wafer crumbs and melted margarine. Set aside 1/4 cup crumbs for garnish.

Pat remaining crumbs into sherbet glasses, pressing firmly.

Chill 3 hours.

Combine frozen lemonade and water. Heat, but DO NOT BOIL. Add marshmallows and stir over low heat, until melted. Chill mixture until cool and syrupy. Whip cream. Fold into mixture, blending well. Pile filling into chilled crumb crust. Garnish with whipped cream and remaining crumbs.

Chill and serve or freeze. When frozen wrap in heavy aluminum foil. Remove from freezer about 30 minutes before serving.

Makes 12 servings.

Grater

The zesty aroma of fresh grated lemon peel enhances many dishes.

The outer skin of the lemon contains lemon oil. It is sometimes called rind or zest, but for simplification it is always lemon peel in this book.

LEMONY RICE PUDDING

1 quart milk
1/2 cup rice
1/2 cup sugar
Peel of 1/2 lemon
1/4 cup raisins
Dash nutmeg

Cook rice with milk over low heat 1 hour. Remove from heat and add sugar, lemon peel, raisins and nutmeg. Refrigerate for several hours to chill and blend flavors. Discard lemon peel when serving.

Makes 8 servings.

SLIVERED PEEL

Score peel of lemon with a knife into quarters. Peel fruit away with fingers. With tip of spoon scrape most of white from peel. Stack 2 pieces at a time on cutting board. Cut into very thin strips.

Scott Forgot
"It is now believed that Captain Scott and his men may have died of scurvy on their expedition to the South Pole in 1912. It seems as though Scott had forgotten the lemons."

The History of Scurvy and Vitamin C, Kenneth Carpenter

LEMON PUFF PUDDING

2 egg whites, stiffly beaten
2 egg yolks, beaten
1/4 cup flour
3/4 cup sugar
1 cup milk
1 lemon, grated peel and juice

Mix flour and sugar. Stir in lemon peel and juice, egg yolks and milk. Fold in stiffly beaten egg whites. Pour into ungreased 1-quart (6-1/2") baking dish or 6 custard cups. Set in pan of 1" deep hot water. Bake at 350 degrees for 45 minutes. Serve upside down.

Makes 6 servings.

This is a favorite recipe I remember my Mom making.

Roll-a-Lemon: *A lemon yields more juice when left at room temperature and rolled on counter top before juicing.*

JEAN'S FRUIT COCKTAIL CAKE

1 can (17 ounces) fruit cocktail,
  drained
2 eggs, separated
1/4 cup flour
1 cup sugar
1 cup milk
1 tablespoon grated lemon peel
1/2 cup lemon juice

Place drained fruit cocktail in bottom of 1-quart baking dish. Beat egg yolks and whites separately. Blend beaten egg yolks, flour, sugar, milk, grated peel and juice together. Fold in stiffly beaten egg whites. Pour mixture over fruit cocktail. Bake in 350 degree oven for 50 minutes or until lightly browned and springs back when tested.

Makes 8 servings.

"The flower of the lemon tree has 5 sepals, 5 petals, numerous stamens and 1 pistel. It is white and pinkish. It has a sweet odor comparable to the orange blossom.
Funk, Wagnalls, 1983

Kids love this!

MAGIC INK
Write a message on paper with lemon juice. Allow it to dry. Hold paper over a candle and the magic message will appear.

LEMON ICE

12 large lemons
Slivered lemon peel of 3 lemons
4 cups water
3 cups sugar

Score lemons. Peel. Sliver the peels of at least 3 lemons. Cut the peeled fruit in half. Remove seeds. Place the fruit and slivered peels in blender container. Blend until smooth. Combine very hot water and sugar. Heat and stir until sugar is dissolved. Stir in lemon puree and peel. Pour mixture into canister of ice cream freezer. Freeze according to manufacturer's directions for freezer.

Makes about 1-1/2 quarts.

LEMON SHERBET

1-1/2 cups sugar
3/4 cup lemon juice
4 cups milk

Mix the sugar and lemon juice. Add milk. The milk may curdle, but after it is frozen it will be smooth. Freeze according to manufacturer's instructions for freezer. Store in covered plastic container in freezer for several hours before serving.

Makes 1-1/4 quarts.

LEMON DELIGHT-A 1954 CLASSIC

1 package lemon jello
1 1/2 cup hot water
1/2 cup evaporated milk
1 cup sugar
2 lemons, grated peel and juice
2 cups graham cracker or cookie crumbs

Dissolve jello in hot water. Chill until syrupy. Whip. Chill milk and whip. Fold jello into whipped milk, add other ingredients. Cover bottom of dish with graham cracker or cookie crumbs. Spoon on the lemon mixture. Sprinkle crumbs over top and chill.

Makes 6 servings.

GARNISH WITH A TWIST OF LEMON FOR AN ELEGANT TOUCH

LOW CAL LEMON ICE CREAM

1 tablespoon margarine
1 tablespoon flour
3-1/4 cups non fat milk
4 packets Equal, each as sweet as
   2 teaspoons sugar
1/2 cup lemon juice
2 teaspoons lemon peel

Melt the margarine in a saucepan. Stir in the flour. Gradually add half the milk, stirring constantly to the boiling point. Cook over low heat 5 minutes. Remove from the heat. Add the rest of the milk. Cool. Turn into a bowl. Add the Equal, lemon juice and peel. Freeze in lemon baskets.

Makes 5 servings.

Serve with sugared pecans.

"Ice cream is the #1 food treat in America." U.S.A. Today
"Pralines 'n Cream is Baskin Robbin's #1 flavor." 6/14/88 U.S.A. Today

LEMON VELVET ICE CREAM

2 cups sugar
2 cups milk
1/2 cup lemon juice
Grated peel of 2 lemons
2 cups heavy cream

Combine sugar and milk. Let stand 1 hour. Add lemon peel and juice. Stir well. Mixture will thicken slightly. Whip cream until stiff. Fold into milk mixture. Pour into freezer can. Follow manufacturer's instructions for freezing.

Makes 8 servings.

This recipe collects compliments!

NEAT TO SERVE
With an ice cream scoop put scoops of frozen desserts on a jelly roll pan or in lemon shells. Freeze until ready to serve.

FRUIT SHERBET

Juice of 3 lemons
Juice of 3 oranges
3 ripe bananas
1 medium can crushed pineapple
1-1/2 cups water
1-1/2 cups sugar

Boil water and sugar 5 minutes. Add other ingredients. Put in freezer can. Follow manufacturer's instructions.

Makes 1-1/2 quarts.

A Citrus Carnival

" A single citrus tree can be turned into a carnival with lemons, limes, grapefruit, tangarines, kumquats, and oranges all ripening on it's branches at the same time."
Oranges by John McPhee

LOW CAL PINEAPPLE SHERBET

1 (8 ounces) can crushed pineapple
4 packets Equal, each as sweet
   as 2 teaspoons sugar
4 cups Mock Buttermilk*
2 tablespoons lemon juice

Mix ingredients. Put in freezer can. Freeze according to manufacturer's instructions. When firm enough scoop with an ice cream scoop. Freeze the scoops in a jelly roll pan in the freezer to make it easier to serve.

Makes 1 quart.

STRAWBERRY SLUSH

1 pint strawberries, washed
and stemmed
1 package (3 ounces) strawberry
gelatin
1/3 cup sugar
1 cup boiling water
2 cups cold water
1/4 cup lemon juice

Mash strawberries. Dissolve gelatin and sugar in boiling water. Stir in remaining ingredients. Pour into shallow pan. Freeze 1 hour or until mixture begins to freeze around edges. Break up frozen mixture with a fork and stir well. Freeze until firm. Let stand at room temperature for about 10 minutes before serving. Stir with fork.

Makes 10 servings.

A refreshing fresh fruit ice that looks and tastes sophisticated but is quick and easy to prepare.

WHITE FONDANT DIPPED STRAWBERRIES

12 large fresh strawberries
1-1/2 cups powdered sugar
1 tablespoon lemon juice
3 tablespoons light corn syrup

In top of double boiler, mix powdered sugar, lemon juice and corn syrup. Cook over hot water. Stir until mixture is smooth and thin enough to coat berries. Remove from heat. Keep fondant warm over hot water. Holding strawberries by hull or stem, dip each into fondant, covering halfway. Place berries on wire rack to dry.

STRAWBERRY LEMON ICE

2 baskets strawberries, washed
  and mashed
3 teaspoons lemon juice
1 mashed banana
1 cup sugar

Blend all together. Put in tray. Freeze. Stir after 1-1/2 hours. Fill lemon boats and cover with plastic wrap. Store in freezer.

Makes 3 cups.

M-m-m-m good........

LEMON BOATS AND SHELLS

To make lemon boats, cut large lemon in half lengthwise. Carefully ream out juice. Scrape shells clean. Edges may be notched or scalloped with kitchen shears. To sit without tipping, cut a thin slice from bottom of each boat. To make lemon shells, cut lemon in half crosswise. Follow above directions.

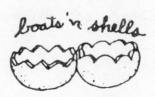

boats 'n shells

WILLIAMSBURG FIG ICE CREAM

4 eggs, separated
1-1/4 cups sugar, divided
2 cups milk, scalded
3 tablespoons lemon juice
1 pint light cream
1/2 cup evaporated milk
1 teaspoon vanilla
1 quart figs, crushed or pureed

Beat egg yolks and half the sugar. Add milk slowly, stirring constantly. Cook over low heat until quite hot, but do not boil. Combine egg whites with remaining sugar. Beat to light froth. Pour egg-milk mixture into egg whites. Stir constantly. Mix in lemon juice. Add cream, milk, vanilla and figs, blending well. Pour mixture into five quart freezer container. Follow directions by manufacturer for freezing. **Do not use eggs with cracked shells.**

Makes 3 quarts.

Milk Equivalents
1 quart evaporated milk = 2 (quart packets) dry powdered milk + 1 quart water
1 pint = 2 cups
1 quart milk = 4 cups milk
1 quart milk = 2 cups evaporated milk + 2 cups water
Sweetened condensed milk = evaporated milk + sugar
Buttermilk = non fat milk in calories
Non fat milk = whole milk with 1/2 the calories

TUTTI FRUTTI ICE CREAM

Juice of 2 lemons
1 envelope unflavored gelatin
1/2 cup hot water
2 cups sugar
1 (8 ounces) jar of maraschino
  cherries and juice
1 (16 ounce) can crushed pineapple
  and juice
1/2 cup chopped nuts
1 can sweetened condensed milk
1 quart whole milk

Add gelatin to lemon juice in blender. Process at lowest speed to soften gelatin. Add hot water. Blend until gelatin is dissolved. Turn to highest speed. Add sugar, cherries and juice. Mix until sugar is dissolved. Put all ingredients in ice cream can. Freeze according to manufacturer's instructions.

Makes 2-1/2 quarts.

ITALIAN DINNER

*Marinated Mushrooms
Mozzarella Cheese and crackers
*Lemon Veal Chops
Spaghetti
Mixed Green Salad with *Creamy Garlic
Dressing
*Herb Lemon Sauce with Zucchini
*Tutti Frutti Ice Cream
*Coffee Napoli

CRANBERRY SHERBET

2 cups cranberries
1 cup water
1 cup sugar
1/4 cup cold water
1 envelope unflavored gelatin
1 lemon, seeded and peeled
1 orange, seeded and peeled

Cook cranberries, water and sugar until skins pop. Put cold water and gelatin into blender container. Add cooked cranberries, lemon and orange. Cover and process until smooth. Put into freezer until mushy. Return to blender. Whip until fluffy. Freeze until firm.

Makes 1 quart.

FRUIT SORBET

2 cups crushed fruit (pineapple, strawberries, raspberries, or apricots)
1/2 cup sugar
1 cup boiling water
3 tablespoons lemon juice

Dissolve sugar in boiling water. Cool syrup. Blend fruit with syrup in food processor or blender. Strain. Press hard on the solids. Add the lemon juice. Chill. Freeze in ice cream maker according to manufacturer's instructions.

Makes 1 pint.

STRAWBERRY ICE CREAM

2 pints fresh strawberries, mashed
1-1/2 cups sugar
2 cans (13 ounces) evaporated milk
1/4 cup lemon juice

Mash berries in blender until pureed. Pour evaporated milk into large mixing bowl. Freeze until ice crystals form along edges. Beat chilled mixture until foamy. Mix in sugar, berries and lemon juice. Beat until mixture doubles in size. Freeze in ice cream freezer following manufacturer's directions.

Makes 1-1/2 quarts.

STRAWBERRY SAUCE

2 cups water
2 cups sugar
2 pints strawberries, stemmed and
    sliced
1/4 cup cornstarch
1/4 cup lemon juice

In saucepan, bring water and sugar to boil. Lower heat. Simmer 3 minutes. Dissolve cornstarch in lemon juice. Stir into sauce. Cook and stir 3 minutes or until sauce is slightly thick and glossy. Cool. Use to glaze fresh strawberry pie or over ice cream.

Makes 1 quart.

Mildew Stains
To remove mildew stains, use lemon juice.
The Caloric Book of Recipes, 1907

BETTY'S LEMON SAUCE

1/2 cup sugar
1 tablespoon cornstarch
1 cup boiling water
2 tablespoons margarine
1-1/2 tablespoons lemon juice
1/8 teaspoon nutmeg

Mix sugar and cornstarch. Add water gradually, stirring constantly. Boil 5 minutes. Remove from heat. Add margarine, lemon juice and nutmeg.
Delicious on top of gingerbread or any cake.

Makes enough for 1 cake.

BILL'S MINCE MEAT SAUCE

1 cup prepared mincemeat
3/4 cup apple juice
1/2 teaspoon grated lemon peel
2 tablespoons lemon juice
1 tablespoon sugar
1/2 teaspoon cornstarch

In a saucepan, combine mincemeat, apple juice and lemon peel. Cook and stir over moderate heat about 5 minutes. Blend lemon juice, sugar and cornstarch. Stir into mincemeat mixture. Simmer until sauce clears and thickens slightly. Serve hot over apple desserts, broiled peach halves and pumpkin pie.

Makes 2 cups.

FLORENCE'S CREAMY CHEESECAKE

1 can pie filling (Blueberry
  or any other flavor)
25 graham crackers (3 cups crumbs)
2/3 cup melted margarine
3 (3 ounce) packages cream cheese
1/3 cup lemon juice
1 (15 ounce) can sweetened condensed
  milk
1 pound sour cream (2 cups)
1 teaspoon vanilla

Use either a 9 x 13" pan with 3/4" sides or an 8" round spring form pan with 3" sides. Crush graham crackers. Mix with 2/3 cup melted margarine. Press onto bottom and sides of pan. Reserve some of the crumbs to sprinkle on top. Spread on pie filling.

Beat cream cheese and condensed milk in mixer until smooth and creamy. Add lemon juice, then sour cream and vanilla. Spoon over pie filling. Sprinkle on reserve crumbs. Bake at 450 degrees for 4 or 5 minutes. Place in freezer to thoroughly chill, (1-1/2 hours) being careful not to let it freeze. Refrigerate until ready to serve.

Makes 12 servings.

...out of this world!

Household Hints
Coarse nets suspended in the store room are very useful for preserving lemons.
The Practical Housekeeper, 1857

PINK LEMONADE PARTY PIE

1 egg
1/4 cup cold water
1 envelope unflavored gelatin
1 can (6 ounces) frozen lemonade
    concentrate
1 can (13 ounces) evaporated milk
Few drops red food color
Graham cracker pie shell

In small saucepan, sprinkle gelatin over water. Let stand 5 minutes to soften. Stir over low heat until gelatin dissolves. Stir in egg. Cook and stir 1 to 2 minutes or until mixture is slightly thickened. Remove from heat. Stir in lemonade concentrate until melted. Chill about 30 minutes or until consistency of unbeaten egg whites. In large bowl beat evaporated milk until soft peaks form. Add lemonade mixture. Continue beating until stiff peaks form. Turn into pie shell. With back of spoon swirl top. Chill at least 1 hour or until set.

Makes 8 servings.

Lemon Bouquet

Fresh lemons on a bed of ivy or other leaves make a refreshing table arrangement.

INDEX

202

GIFT IDEAS

A copy of **LEMON TWIST**
(alone or with any of the below)

ORDER SEVERAL FOR PERFECT GIFTS ANYTIME

Nutrition Unlimited Publications
P.O. Box 701--Arcadia,CA 91006

Please send____copies of **Lemon Twist** at $14.95
each. CA residents add $.95 Enclose $2.50
shipping and handling charges for each book.
Enclosed is a check or money order for:_____.

Name_____.

Address_____Apt._____.

City_____State_____Zip_____.

Make check payable to Nutrition Unlimited
Publications.

PASS THIS CARD ON TO A FRIEND

NUTRITION UNLIMITED PUBLICATIONS
P.O. Box 701--Arcadia, CA 91006

Please send____copies of **Lemon Twist** at
$14.95 each. CA residents add $.95. Enclose
$2.50 shipping and handling charges for each
book.
Enclosed is a check or money order for:

Name_____.

Address_____Apt._____.

City_____State_____Zip_____.

Make check payable to Nutrition Unlimited
Publications.